OECD Public Governance Reviews

OECD Guidelines for Citizen Participation Processes

This document, as well as any data and map included herein, are without prejudice to the status of or sovereignty over any territory, to the delimitation of international frontiers and boundaries and to the name of any territory, city or area.

The statistical data for Israel are supplied by and under the responsibility of the relevant Israeli authorities. The use of such data by the OECD is without prejudice to the status of the Golan Heights, East Jerusalem and Israeli settlements in the West Bank under the terms of international law.

Note by the Republic of Türkiye
The information in this document with reference to "Cyprus" relates to the southern part of the Island. There is no single authority representing both Turkish and Greek Cypriot people on the Island. Türkiye recognises the Turkish Republic of Northern Cyprus (TRNC). Until a lasting and equitable solution is found within the context of the United Nations, Türkiye shall preserve its position concerning the "Cyprus issue".

Note by all the European Union Member States of the OECD and the European Union
The Republic of Cyprus is recognised by all members of the United Nations with the exception of Türkiye. The information in this document relates to the area under the effective control of the Government of the Republic of Cyprus.

Please cite this publication as:
OECD (2022), *OECD Guidelines for Citizen Participation Processes*, OECD Public Governance Reviews, OECD Publishing, Paris, https://doi.org/10.1787/f765caf6-en.

ISBN 978-92-64-53294-6 (print)
ISBN 978-92-64-66299-5 (pdf)
ISBN 978-92-64-77030-0 (HTML)
ISBN 978-92-64-94435-0 (epub)

OECD Public Governance Reviews
ISSN 2219-0406 (print)
ISSN 2219-0414 (online)

Photo credits: Cover © Ryoji Iwata via Unsplash.

Corrigenda to publications may be found on line at: www.oecd.org/about/publishing/corrigenda.htm.
© OECD 2022

The use of this work, whether digital or print, is governed by the Terms and Conditions to be found at https://www.oecd.org/termsandconditions.

Foreword

Citizen and stakeholder participation is an essential element of an open government, and is recognised as such by Provisions 8 and 9 of the OECD Recommendation of the Council on Open Government (2017). Open government is defined by the OECD as "a culture of governance that promotes the principles of transparency, integrity, accountability and stakeholder participation in support of democracy and inclusive growth". The concept is based on the idea that citizens and the public should be enabled to see, understand, contribute to, monitor, and evaluate public decisions and actions. Open government can increase the legitimacy of public decision making and improve its outcomes, by informing and involving citizens - including those usually underrepresented - and by answering to people's real needs. In the long term, open government reforms can help foster trust in government and reinforce democracy.

Citizens[1] today are more informed than ever and are demanding a say in shaping the policies and services that affect their lives. In response, public institutions at all levels of government are increasingly creating opportunities to harness citizens' experiences and knowledge to make better public decisions. The global landscape for citizen and stakeholder participation is evolving constantly, becoming richer with new and innovative ways to involve citizens and stakeholders in public decisions. At the same time, differences of involving these two groups have become apparent, as individual citizens require participation methods designed to provide them with time, information, resources, and incentives needed to engage, while stakeholders (any interested and/or affected party, such as institutions and organisations) have a lower participation threshold, dedicated resources, and clear interests to participate.

Many of the existing resources in the field focus on stakeholder participation. These guidelines aim to fill a void by providing practical, hands-on support to organise citizen participation processes in particular, highlighting specific considerations and providing dedicated methods with an emphasis on ensuring quality, inclusion, and impact. The content of these guidelines is based on evidence collected by the OECD over the years, the OECD *Handbook on Information, Consultation and Public Participation in Policy-Making* (2001), the OECD Recommendation on Open Government (2017), the OECD *Handbook on Open Government for Peruvian Public Servants* (2020), the OECD *Report on Innovative Citizen Participation and New Democratic Institutions: Catching the Deliberative Wave* (2020), the OECD and DG REGIO *Citizen Participation in Cohesion Policy Guidelines and Playbooks* (2022), as well as existing resources from academia and other organisations.

The guidelines walk the reader through ten steps to design, plan, and implement a citizen participation process, and detail seven different methods that can be used to involve citizens in policy making. To illustrate these methods, the OECD gathered good practice examples through an open call. As part of this document, the OECD suggests nine guiding principles that help ensure the quality of these processes.

The OECD *Guidelines for Citizen Participation Processes* is a tool for any individual or organisation interested in designing, planning, and implementing a citizen participation process, such as policy makers,

---

[1] The term is meant in the larger sense of 'an inhabitant of a particular place', which can be in reference to a village, town, city, region, state, or country depending on the context. It is not meant in the more restrictive sense of 'a legally recognised national of a state'. In this larger sense, it is equivalent of people.

practitioners, as well as civil society organisations, citizens, the private sector, or academia. The OECD looks forward to further collaboration with Member and Partner Countries in the implementation of the good practices and principles included in these Guidelines. This document was approved by the Public Governance Committee via written procedure on September 2, 2022 and prepared for publication by the OECD Secretariat.

Acknowledgements

The OECD Secretariat wishes to express its gratitude and acknowledge all the institutions and individuals that have contributed to these Guidelines. This document was prepared by the OECD Public Governance Directorate (GOV) under the leadership of Elsa Pilichowski. It was drafted under the strategic direction of Alessandro Bellantoni, Head of the Open Government and Civic Space Unit and Claudia Chwalisz, Innovative Citizen Participation Lead. The Guidelines were written by Ieva Česnulaitytė and Mauricio Mejía. José Sánchez Ruiz provided support throughout the drafting process. Alessandro Bellantoni, Claudia Chwalisz, and David Goessmann provided strategic comments throughout the document.

The Guidelines benefited from feedback provided by delegates to the OECD Public Governance Committee, the OECD Working Party on Open Government, and members of the Innovative Citizen Participation Network (ICPN), and the OECD Network on Open and Innovative Government in Latin America and the Caribbean:

Jérôme Bétrancourt (Nos vies, nos avis, New Caledonia), Marta Crespo (Government of Spain), Ninoschka Dante (Government of Uruguay), Tania Da Rosa (Government of Uruguay), Marjan Ehsassi (Johns Hopkins University, United States), Jayne Foster (Government of New Zealand), Priscilla Haueisen Ruas (Government of Brazil), José Hernández (InfoCDMX, Mexico), Katju Holkeri (Government of Finland), Matina Lekka (Government of Greece), Victoria Lozano Muñoz (Government of Spain), Otavio Morerira de Castro Neves (Government of Brazil), Paul Natorp (Sager der Samler, Denmark), Emma Obermair (People Powered, United States), Anastasios Papazarifis (Government of Greece), Jana Tichackova (Government of Czech Republic), Nicolas Valencia Sierra (Government of Colombia), Fabiola Vidal (Government of Chile), Constanza Velásquez (Government of Chile).

In addition, the drafting team would like to thank those OECD colleagues that provided comments, namely: Alessandro Bozzini, Emma Cantera, Claire McEvoy, Bruno Monteiro, Carla Musi, Chiara Varazzani, Michaela Sullivan-Paul, and Joshua Yeremiyew for the administrative support. Lastly, we would like to acknowledge the colleagues that reviewed this publication as part of the Editorial Board process: Gillian Dorner, Edwin Lau, and Gregor Virant.

Table of contents

Foreword	3
Acknowledgements	5
Reader's guide	9
Executive summary	10

1 Citizen participation: Why and when to involve citizens?   12

What are citizen and stakeholder participation? Key terms	13
What are the differences between involving stakeholders and citizens?	14
Why involve citizens?	16
How can citizen participation support public authorities and institutions?	16
Myths about citizen participation	17
References	19

2 Planning, implementing, and evaluating a citizen participation process   20

Should I involve citizens?	21
Ten-step path of planning and implementing a citizen participation process	21
Step 1: Identifying the problem to solve and the moment for participation	22
Step 2: Defining the expected objectives and results	25
Step 3: Identifying the relevant group of people to involve and recruiting participants	26
Step 4: Choosing the participation method	30
Step 5: Choosing the right digital tools	51
Step 6: Communicating about the process	53
Step 7: Implementing a participatory process	56
Step 8: Using citizen input and providing feedback	60
Step 9: Evaluating the participation process	61
Step 10: Fostering a culture of participation	62
References	64

3 Ensuring quality of participation: Guiding Principles for Citizen Participation Processes   66

Guiding principles for citizen participation processes	67
References	70

4 Useful resources   71

Databases of various examples of citizen participation	72

Handbooks & further readings on citizen and stakeholder participation	72
OECD publications	72
Good practice principles	72
Blogs and podcasts	73
Resources on how to identify a public problem	73
Resources on identifying participants and recruitment processes	73
Resources on using digital tools for participation	73
Resources on communication	74
Resources on inclusion and accessibility	74
Resources on evaluation	74
Resources and guidance on open meetings / Townhall meetings	74
Resources and guidance on public consultations	75
Resources and guidance on open innovation	77
Resources and guidance on citizen science	78
Resources and guidance on civic monitoring	79
Resources and guidance on participatory budgeting	80
Resources and guidance on representative deliberative processes	82

5 Checklist for designing and planning a citizen participation process — 85

FIGURES

Figure 1.1. Three pillars of participation	14
Figure 2.1. Ten-step path for planning and implementing a citizen participation process	22
Figure 2.2. Stages of the decision or policy cycle, and the potential role of citizens	23
Figure 2.3. How to run a civic lottery?	28
Figure 2.4. What is a representative deliberative process?	49
Figure 2.5. Citizens' journey through a participatory process	59
Figure 3.1. Guiding Principles for Citizen Participation Processes	67

TABLES

Table 1.1. Differences between involving citizens and stakeholders	15
Table 2.1. Types of inputs or contributions from citizens and the expected impact on public decisions	25
Table 2.2. Examples of identifying the target public and choosing recruitment type	27
Table 2.3. Citizen participation methods: Comparing key characteristics	30
Table 2.4. Types of public consultations	38
Table 2.5. Typology of civic monitoring mechanisms	44
Table 2.6. Selecting the right digital tool for citizen participation	52
Table 2.7. How to communicate during a participatory process?	53
Table 4.1. Steps of an open meeting/town hall meeting	75
Table 4.2. Steps of a public consultation	76
Table 4.3. Steps for Open Innovation	77
Table 4.4. Steps for Citizen Science	78
Table 4.5. Steps for implementing a civic monitoring process	79
Table 4.6. Steps for implementing a participatory budget	80
Table 4.7. Steps of a representative deliberative process	82

Reader's guide

These guidelines consist of four chapters:

1. **Chapter 1** defines citizen participation, outlines reasons to involve citizens in public decision making, and addresses the most common myths about citizen participation.

2. **Chapter 2** introduces a ten-step path for planning and implementing a citizen participation process and provides detailed advice and instructions for how to do it. The path takes the reader through a process of reflection, starting from the problem that the participation process will address, all the way through to choosing the most applicable participation method, recruiting participants, choosing the appropriate tools, setting the timeline, communicating, ensuring inclusivity, evaluating it, and more. At the end of each step, the guidelines provide helpful questions for reflection. **Annex A** contains a checklist that can be used to guide the reader through the implementation of a participatory process. This chapter is most helpful for policy makers who would like to implement a participatory process, but are not sure where to start, which method to use, or who to involve.

3. **Chapter 3** suggests nine guiding principles to help ensure the quality of participatory processes.

4. **Chapter 4** provides further resources on citizen participation, which include relevant OECD and external publications and databases with relevant participation examples, and participation handbooks. This chapter provides guidance on each participation method covered in the guidelines

5. **Chapter 5** is a checklist that summarises the ten steps suggested by these guidelines.

6. The advice and methods outlined in these four chapters can be used by a wide variety of actors for different purposes.

- **Senior public officials and government policy makers** can use the guidelines to shape their institutions' agendas and to apply citizen participation methods to the policies and services they design and implement.
- **Any public official** can use these guidelines to make concrete contributions to their institution's citizen participation vision and efforts.
- **Local governments** can find inspiration for citizen participation processes that can be adapted to their context and help promote citizen participation within their own spheres of responsibility.
- **Any citizen or civil society organisation** can use these guidelines to learn about different ways their governments can involve them in public decision making and make their preferences for increased participation known.
- **Other actors, such as academics or private companies,** can apply these methods to involve citizens in their research or other activities.

Executive summary

These are guidelines for any individual or organisation interested in designing, planning, and implementing a citizen participation process. The guidelines walk the reader through ten practical steps, and detail eight different methods that can be used to involve citizens in policy making. This publication is illustrated with good practice examples.

Citizen participation has intrinsic and instrumental benefits. It leads to a better and more democratic policy-making process, which becomes more transparent, inclusive, legitimate, and accountable. It enhances public trust in government and democratic institutions by giving citizens a role in public decision making. By taking into account and using citizens' experience and knowledge, it helps public institutions tackle complex policy problems and leads to better policy results.

Ten-step path of planning and implementing a citizen participation process

Citizen participation processes should be organised only when there is room for meaningful citizen participation in the decision-making process. A ten-step path was developed to provide guidance along the way:

1. **Identifying the problem to solve and the moment for participation:** The first step when planning a citizen participation process is to identify if there is a genuine problem that the public can help solve. If there is, then the problem needs to be defined and framed as a question. Citizens can be actively involved in any of the stages or throughout the policy cycle: when identifying the issue, formulating policy, making decisions, implementing policy, or evaluating it.

2. **Defining the expected results:** A clear understanding of the expected outcomes or results of the participation process is needed to define the desired inputs or contributions from citizens and the impact they will have on the final decision.

3. **Identifying the relevant group of people to involve and recruiting participants:** Different types of groups can be involved in a participation process, such as a broad group of citizens from diverse backgrounds, a representative group of citizens, a particular community based on geography or other demographic characteristics, as well as stakeholders, ranging from non-governmental organisations to businesses or academia. Different strategies can be employed to recruit them – an open call, a closed call, or a civic lottery.

4. **Choosing the participation method:** Eight citizen participation methods and their characteristics are compared and described to help choose the most applicable one in a given situation: information and communication, open meetings/town hall meetings, civic monitoring, public consultation, open innovation, citizen science, participatory budgeting, and representative deliberative processes.

5. **Choosing the right digital tools:** Digital tools can allow citizens and stakeholders to interact and submit their inputs in different ways. They should be chosen to facilitate the participation method.

Policy makers should keep in mind the existing "digital divides", plan for technical, human, and financial resources needed to deploy digital tools, and choose tools that are transparent and accountable. When possible, digital tools should be chosen alongside in-person methods.

6. **Communicating about the process:** Public communication can help at every step of the way – from recruiting citizens, to ensuring the transparency of the process, to extending the benefits of learning about a specific policy issue to the broader public. Constant, clear, and understandable communication that uses plain language is most effective.

7. **Implementing the participation process:** There are general considerations that concern the implementation of any participatory process: preparing an adequate timeline, identifying the needed resources, ensuring inclusion and accessibility, and considering a citizens' journey through a participatory process.

8. **Using citizen input and providing feedback:** The inputs received as part of the participatory process should be given careful and respectful consideration and used as stipulated in the beginning – with clear justifications if any inputs or recommendations are not used or implemented. Communicating to participants about the status of their inputs and the ultimate outcome of their participation helps to close the feedback loop.

9. **Evaluating the participation process:** Through evaluation, the quality and neutrality of a participatory process can be measured and demonstrated to the broader public. Evaluation also creates an opportunity for learning by providing evidence and lessons for public authorities and practitioners about what went well, and what did not.

10. **Fostering a culture of participation:** A shift from ad hoc participation processes to a culture of participation can be supported by embedding institutionalised participation mechanisms, multiplying opportunities for citizens to exercise their democratic "muscles" beyond participation, and protecting a vibrant civic space.

Guiding principles for quality citizen participation processes

The methods of citizen participation outlined in these guidelines rely on principles of good practice to ensure their quality: **clarity and impact, commitment and accountability, transparency, inclusiveness and accessibility, integrity, privacy, information, resources,** and **evaluation**.

1 Citizen participation: Why and when to involve citizens?

This chapter sets the scene for citizen and stakeholder participation in public decision making. It introduces the key concepts and terms, and makes the case for public authorities to involve citizens more regularly and more meaningfully. It builds on the OECD Recommendation of the Council on Open Government.

What are citizen and stakeholder participation? Key terms

Conceptually, there are different terms used to refer to citizen involvement in public decisions: citizen engagement, public participation, civic participation, etc. When defining participation, the OECD Recommendation on Open Government (2017[1]) refers to stakeholders, grouping together both citizens and any interested and/or affected party. Involving citizens and/or stakeholders is equally important, however, their participation should not be treated identically (OECD, 2022[2]). When referring to these groups, the following distinction can be made:

- **Stakeholders**: any interested and/or affected party, including institutions and organisations, whether governmental or non-governmental, from civil society, academia, the media, or the private sector.
- **Citizens**: individuals, regardless of their age, gender, sexual orientation, religious, and political affiliations. The term is meant in the larger sense of 'an inhabitant of a particular place', which can be in reference to a village, town, city, region, state, or country depending on the context. It is not meant in the more restrictive sense of 'a legally recognised national of a state'. In this larger sense, it is equivalent of people.

These guidelines acknowledge the diversity of concepts, and employs the term of citizen and stakeholder participation, which allows to make a distinction between the two groups and put emphasis on citizen participation practices in particular.

Citizen and stakeholder participation includes "all the ways in which stakeholders (including citizens) can be involved in the policy cycle and in service design and delivery" (OECD, 2017[1]). It refers to the efforts by public institutions to hear the views, perspectives, and inputs from citizens and stakeholders. Participation allows citizens and stakeholders to influence the activities and decisions of public authorities at different stages of the policy cycle.

The OECD Recommendation of the Council on Open Government (2017) distinguishes among three levels of citizen and stakeholder participation, which differ according to the level of involvement:

- **Information:** an initial level of participation characterised by a one-way relationship in which the government produces and delivers information to citizens and stakeholders. It covers both on-demand provision of information and "proactive" measures by the government to disseminate information.
- **Consultation:** a more advanced level of participation that entails a two-way relationship in which citizens and stakeholders provide feedback to the government and vice-versa. It is based on the prior definition of the issue for which views are being sought and requires the provision of relevant information, in addition to feedback on the outcomes of the process.
- **Engagement:** when citizens and stakeholders are given the opportunity and the necessary resources (e.g., information, data, and digital tools) to collaborate during all phases of the policy-cycle and in the service design and delivery. It acknowledges equal standing for citizens in setting the agenda, proposing project or policy options and shaping the dialogue – although the responsibility for the final decision or policy formulation in many cases rests with public authorities.

Figure 1.1. Three pillars of participation

1. INFORMATION
- Initial level of participation
- One-way relationship
- On-demand provision of information
- Proactive measures to disseminate information

2. CONSULTATION
- More advanced
- Two-way relationship
- Requires provision of information plus feedback on outcomes of process

3. ENGAGEMENT
- When stakeholders (including citizens + civil society) are given opportunity and necessary resources to collaborate during all phases of the policy-cycle and in service design + delivery

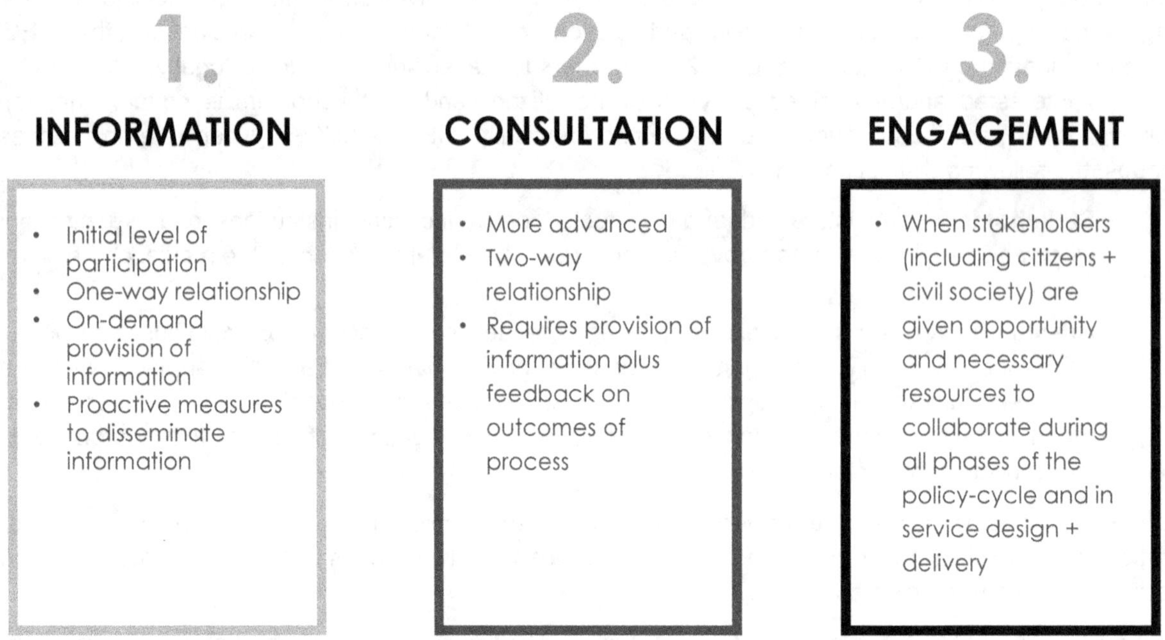

Source: Author's own elaboration based on OECD Recommendation of the Council on Open Government (2017[1])

These guidelines acknowledge that in addition to the OECD pillars of participation, policymakers and institutions have adopted the IAP2's Spectrum of Public Participation (2018[3]) which measures participation in relation to the impact it has on the decisions using five stages.

The OECD Guidelines for Citizen Participation Processes cover all three levels of participation; however, they focus on the second and third levels: **consultation** and **engagement**.

What are the differences between involving stakeholders and citizens?

These guidelines focus mainly on **citizen participation**, since stakeholder participation is usually more familiar to policy makers and requires less specialised knowledge (as detailed in Table 1.1). Citizen and stakeholder participation are also not mutually exclusive – stakeholders often have a role in designing, implementing, or providing their perspectives during a citizen participation process. Some methods included in these guidelines can be adapted to both types of participants. For example, public consultations can be used to involve both stakeholders and citizens.

The line between these groups can be blurry and, in reality, is not always perfectly neat. No value or preference is given to citizens or stakeholders in particular, as both groups can enrich public decisions, projects, policies, and services. However, public authorities should decide whom to engage at which stage of decision making, and then adapt the design and expectations of the participatory process in accordance with the category of participants. Individual citizens and stakeholders will not require the same conditions to participate and will not produce the same types of inputs. Stakeholders can provide expertise and more specific input than citizens through mechanisms such as advisory bodies or experts' panels, whereas citizen participation requires methods that provide the public with the time, information, and resources to produce quality inputs and develop individual or collective recommendations. Both require a clear link to decision making.

Table 1.1. Differences between involving citizens and stakeholders

	Involving stakeholders	Involving citizens
Definition	Stakeholders - any interested and/or affected party, including institutions and organisations, whether governmental or non-governmental, from civil society, academia, the media, or the private sector.	Citizens - individuals, regardless of their age, gender, sexual orientation, religious and political affiliations, or any other condition - in the larger sense 'an inhabitant of a particular place', which can be in reference to a village, town, city, region, state, or country depending on the context.
Potential benefits of involvement	<ul><li>Brings in official stakeholder perspectives</li><li>Yields expert opinion and knowledge, can point to relevant evidence and studies</li><li>Ensures representation of key actors</li><li>Depending on the type of stakeholder, can help raise awareness and facilitate public learning about an issue</li><li>Helps to identify potential impacts, deliver tailor made solutions, and ensure their effectiveness</li><li>Depending on the type of stakeholder, can help mobilise support and resources needed to implement a policy or an initiative</li><li>Builds on existing networks or partnerships</li></ul>	<ul><li>Brings in public opinion or public judgement</li><li>Can bring a diversity of views and include rarely heard voices</li><li>Can be representative of the broader public (if a representative group is engaged)</li><li>Helps raise awareness and facilitates public learning about an issue</li><li>Helps to identify potential impacts, deliver tailor-made solutions, and ensure their effectiveness</li><li>Facilitates building social cohesion and a greater sense of community</li><li>Strengthens democratic institutions</li></ul>
Considerations when preparing to involve	<ul><li>Threshold to participate is low</li><li>Have dedicated time and resources for getting informed about the issue and to participate</li><li>Often have clear interest and incentives to participate</li><li>Often have experience interacting with public authorities and having a role in the decision-making process</li><li>Important to avoid policy capture by certain influential groups or individual interests</li></ul>	<ul><li>Threshold to participate is high</li><li>Do not have dedicated time and resources for getting informed about the issue and to participate – these conditions should be built into the design of the participation process</li><li>Often do not have personal interest or incentives to participate. Their motivation to participate should be ignited (for example, by designing an inviting participation process)</li><li>Often do not have a strong sense that they can have an impact on decisions. This sense should be nurtured by establishing clear links to decision making, invitations from high-level figures</li></ul>

Source: Author's own elaboration based on OECD's Innovative Citizen Participation and New Democratic Institutions: Catching the Deliberative Wave (2020[4]).

Why involve citizens?

It is good for democracy

As a core pillar of an open government, citizen participation has intrinsic benefits. It leads to better and more democratic policy making, which becomes more transparent, inclusive, legitimate, and accountable. Citizen participation enhances public trust in government and democratic institutions by giving citizens a role in public decision making. It also leads to a better shared understanding of opportunities and challenges.

It is good for policies, services, and projects

Citizen participation also has instrumental benefits. It leads to better policy results that take into account and use citizens' experience and knowledge to address citizens' most pressing needs. The quality of policies, laws, and services is improved, as they were developed, implemented, and evaluated based on up-to-date evidence and a well-informed policy choice could be made. They also benefit from the innovative ideas of citizens and can be more cost-effective as a result (OECD, 2016[5]).

It is good for inclusion and diversity

Citizen participation can make governance and decision making more inclusive by opening the door to more representative groups of people. Through participatory processes, public authorities can include the voice of the "silent majority" and strengthen the representation of minorities and often excluded groups like informal workers, migrants, women, indigenous populations, LGBTI communities, etc. Citizen participation in public decision making can answer the concerns of minorities and unrepresented groups by addressing inequalities of voice and access, and thus fight exclusion and marginalisation. This in turn can create better policies and services, build a sense of belonging, and foster social cohesion (OECD, 2020[6]).

It is good for legitimacy and facilitates implementation

Involving citizens in the decision-making process supports the public understanding of the outcome and enhances its uptake. Citizen participation can allow the public to follow, influence, and understand the process leading to a decision, which in turn enhances the legitimacy of hard choices and social support for change. Empowering citizens through participatory processes is also good for the overall legitimacy of the democratic process as it signals civic respect and builds a relationship based on mutual trust.

Citizen participation is a right

The right of citizens to participate in public decision making and service design and delivery can be rooted in international agreements, in the constitution, or in specific legislation. This right can be broad (e.g. citizens should have a say in decisions that affect their lives); it can be specific to certain types of decisions (e.g. environmental decisions or urban planning); or refer to a specific participatory method (e.g. referendum or consultations). The OECD *Guiding Principles for Open and Inclusive Policy Making* (OECD, 2009[7]) invite countries to firmly ground citizens' right to participate in law or policy to ensure its institutionalisation and sustainability.

How can citizen participation support public authorities and institutions?

Citizen participation can support the daily activities of public servants as well as public institutions' decision-making processes (OECD, 2022[8]).

Citizen participation can help public authorities solve problems or address specific situations, such as:

- Public problems that require careful consideration from a diversity of perspectives;
- When there is a vacuum of ideas and solutions;
- Addressing complex issues that require informed public judgment;
- Navigating trade-offs and setting priorities;
- Preparing long-term plans.

Citizen participation can help public authorities in their daily activities to take better decisions and provide services and policies that respond to citizens' needs, especially:

- As a way to gather information, data, and public opinion;
- As an opportunity to tap into the collective intelligence to co-create solutions, services, or projects;
- As a mechanism to collect public feedback on proposed solutions such as draft legislation or plans;
- As a tool to adapt and design public services that respond the real needs of citizens;
- To involve citizens and stakeholders in the implementation of policies, projects, and research.
- As a tool to understand costs, benefits, or impacts of policy decisions on specific communities that might have escaped the initial considerations and analysis;
- To prevent conflict situations that might arise from not considering the needs of all relevant groups.

Citizen participation can increase the legitimacy of decision making and promote a relationship between citizens and public authorities based on mutual trust:

- By engaging with citizens in a meaningful and more regular way beyond the ballot box;
- By allowing citizens to experience and understand how decisions are taken, which in turn can increase confidence in the final decision;
- When more advanced engagement methods are used, by sharing the decision-making power with citizens, showing a sense of respect, and cultivating a sense of empowerment.

Myths about citizen participation

There are several common myths and misconceptions about citizen participation:

Citizens are not capable of understanding the complexity of an issue or project.

Often people who are experts in a specific field have spent many years gaining experience and knowledge to understand a complex issue. While citizens are often not as knowledgeable about a subject as experts, there is a large amount of evidence which shows that citizens are able to grapple with complexity if the process has been designed to give them time and resources for learning (OECD, 2020[4]; Mercier and Landemore, 2012[9]; Grönlund, Herne and Setälä, 2015[10]). Experts should be involved in helping select, prepare, and present broad and diverse information for citizens to be able to develop *informed* recommendations.

Decision makers, whether elected representatives or appointed officials, are not experts on all topics on which they are required to take decisions either. A member of parliament cannot be a specialist on every single policy issue covered by legislation. They have access to technical experts that guide them in understanding complex problems. This can – and should – also be the case for citizens.

Citizens are unreliable and will not commit fully to the participation process.

Another common misconception is that citizens will either not participate, or will drop out partway through a process. Sometimes there is a sense that we ask too much of people, however, more often than not, we ask *too little*. Evidence shows that people are not only willing to participate, but they are ambitious, driven, and will work hard to achieve goals *if they see that the process is worth their time and effort, with a clear link to impact* (OECD, 2020[4]).

To make it worthwhile, there must be a clear link to the decision-making process, meaning that citizens' recommendations, ideas, and proposals will be considered by a public authority or another actor in charge of making decisions. It should be clear how and when the public authority will use those inputs and will provide a direct response to citizens.

Citizen participation levels are also affected by the design of a participation exercise. A good design will help overcome barriers to participation by:

- giving citizens a clear task;
- being transparent about the process and its intended impact;
- providing an opportunity for learning;
- giving enough information for people to come to an informed point of view;
- having well-moderated, well-facilitated dialogue and deliberation;
- and providing compensation for time/travel/other costs.

It is helpful to ask yourself: *"Would I be motivated to take part in my participatory process? Is it clear what is asked of me and that my time is worth the effort?"* If your process is well designed, the answer to both questions should be yes. Further guidance on this is provided in the *How to incentivise citizens to participate?* and *Thinking as a citizen* sections of this report.

Citizens will develop either a wish list or a list of grievances.

This myth is based on the negative past experiences of interacting with citizens in participatory processes. Often public servants face citizens in situations such as a town hall meeting or a public consultation where people are just generally asked to provide comments or feedback. In such circumstances, usually citizens with something negative to say show up to express a complaint or disagree with a public decision, because the process is designed this way.

However, participation can be designed to elicit constructive contributions towards finding solutions and building consensus. If a citizen participation process is designed to gather ideas, co-develop solutions, or co-implement activities or policies, citizens will do just that – they will work in a constructive, meaningful way.

It is possible that citizens might initially use participatory processes to express frustration about other problems they have faced that they feel public authorities are responsible for or could help address. In such cases, citizens could be guided towards appropriate channels where they could address their complaints or find help for solving issues experienced.

References

Grönlund, K., K. Herne and M. Setälä (2015), "Does Enclave Deliberation Polarize Opinions?", *Political Behavior*, Vol. 37/4, pp. 995-1020, https://doi.org/10.1007/s11109-015-9304-x. [10]

International Association for Public Participation (2018), *IAP2 Spectrum of Public Participation*, https://iap2.org.au/wp-content/uploads/2020/01/2018_IAP2_Spectrum.pdf. [3]

Mercier, H. and H. Landemore (2012), "Reasoning Is for Arguing: Understanding the Successes and Failures of Deliberation", *Political Psychology*, Vol. 33/2, pp. 243-258, https://doi.org/10.1111/j.1467-9221.2012.00873.x. [9]

OECD (2022), "Engaging citizens in cohesion policy: DG REGIO and OECD pilot project final report", *OECD Working Papers on Public Governance*, No. 50, OECD Publishing, Paris, https://doi.org/10.1787/486e5a88-en. [8]

OECD (2022), *Open Government Review of Brazil: Towards and Integrated Open Government Agenda*. [2]

OECD (2020), *INCLUSIVE SOCIAL DIALOGUE AND CITIZEN ENGAGEMENT TO ENHANCE SOCIAL COHESION AND OWNERSHIP OF RECOVERY MEASURES*. [6]

OECD (2020), *Innovative Citizen Participation and New Democratic Institutions: Catching the Deliberative Wave*, OECD Publishing, Paris, https://doi.org/10.1787/339306da-en. [4]

OECD (2017), *Recommendation of the Council on Open Government*, http://acts.oecd.orgRECOMMENDATIONPUBLICGOVERNANCE (accessed on 18 February 2022). [1]

OECD (2016), *Open Government: The Global Context and the Way Forward*, OECD Publishing, Paris, https://doi.org/10.1787/9789264268104-en. [5]

OECD (2009), *Focus on Citizens: Public Engagement for Better Policy and Services*, OECD Studies on Public Engagement, OECD Publishing, Paris, https://doi.org/10.1787/9789264048874-en. [7]

2 Planning, implementing, and evaluating a citizen participation process

This chapter introduces a ten-step path for planning, implementing, and evaluating a citizen participation process. It provides guidance on how to implement each step, and details eight participatory methods from information to deliberative processes. This chapter illustrates the steps and the methods with good practices from OECD member and partner countries.

Should I involve citizens?

Citizen participation processes should be organised only when there is room for meaningful citizen participation in the decision-making process. Participation processes initiated by a public authority that do not lead to a meaningful contribution to policy making or lack substance, time, or other resources to be well-implemented risk disappointing citizens and compromising their trust in government.

Citizens should only be involved in a decision-making process if:

- There is a problem that citizens can help solve.
- There is room in the decision-making process for citizens to have influence over certain decisions. In other words, it is possible to act on the advice received from people.
- There is a genuine commitment by senior leadership to take into account citizens' inputs.
- There are sufficient financial, technical, and human resources available to implement a meaningful participatory process.
- There is enough time to organise a participatory process, and the timeframe fits the decision-making cycle. Meaning that the decision has not been taken before the process starts.

Or when there is legislation that mandates citizen participation in a particular situation. In such cases the conditions above should also be in place for the citizen participation process to be fruitful.

Ten-step path of planning and implementing a citizen participation process

To support public authorities, the OECD has developed a ten-step path to planning, implementing, and evaluating a citizen participation process. The objective is to provide guidance and advice throughout the different important steps, and ensure that the process designed is inviting, with the right public in mind, and using an appropriate participation method. Emphasis is put on ensuring quality, inclusion, and impact. Nevertheless, these guidelines do not aim at being prescriptive, and acknowledge that there might be other steps, or other paths to follow.

These guidelines encourage the readers to involve potential participants - when possible - in the early design of the participatory process to ensure it works for them, and to increase the level of participation.

This chapter outlines the suggested ten steps and provides details and advice for each.

Figure 2.1. Ten-step path for planning and implementing a citizen participation process

Source: Author's own elaboration based on Faulkner and Bynner (2020[1]), How to Design and Plan Public Engagement Processes: A Handbook, Glasgow. What Works Scotland; Involve (2005[2]) People & Participation: How to put citizens at the heart of decision-making, London: Beacon Press, and New Zealand Government (2022[3]), Community Engagement Policy Tool, The Policy Project.

Step 1: Identifying the problem to solve and the moment for participation

Citizen participation can be helpful to address problems in most policy areas, from climate change, public health, housing, infrastructure, transportation, education, to combating inequality and social exclusion, among others. Regardless of the policy area, **the first step when planning a citizen participation process is to identify if there is a genuine problem that the public can help solve. If there is, then the problem needs to be defined and framed as a question or issue.** Defining a precise problem or question is one of the most important elements of successfully engaging citizens, as it gives them a clear ask with a clear task.

It is also important to be clear about the stage of the decision-making process in which citizens' inputs are most valuable and can have influence. Clarity about the problem and the timing will then help define the type of input that is needed, the type of participants that should be involved, and the most appropriate method to engage them.

How to identify the problem the public can help solve?

Identifying and detailing the problem citizens will help solve, or the question that they will answer is the start of designing a participatory process. A poorly defined problem is much more difficult to solve, as the way a problem or situation is understood and framed has an impact on the range and types of possible solutions (OECD, 2019[4]).

Public authorities can answer the following questions to help identify the precise problem citizens can help address:

- Is the problem you are tackling clearly defined?
- Is there agreement about the problem between different actors?
- Is there certainty about the nature of the problem?
- Is the problem likely to stay the same throughout the problem-solving process?
- Are there existing, generally accepted solutions?
- Is there previous experience tackling this problem?
- If the problem or the challenge is broad, what are some of the smaller problems the public can help address?
- What do you want to learn from participants that you don't already know?
- What do you expect from involving citizens? Is it ideas how to solve your problem? Ready-to-implement solutions? Opinions and feedback about possible solutions?
- What precise problem or challenge will participants help solve?

At what stages of the decision or policy cycle can citizens be involved?

The decision-making or policy cycle is usually composed of five stages: issue identification; policy or project formulation; decision making; implementation; and evaluation (OECD, 2016[5]). It is indispensable, throughout all stages, to provide citizens with clear and relevant information. Beyond this, citizens can be actively involved in any of the following stages or throughout the cycle.

Figure 2.2. Stages of the decision or policy cycle, and the potential role of citizens

Source: Author's own elaboration based on (OECD, 2016[5]), Open Government: The Global Context and the Way Forward, OECD Publishing, Paris, https://doi.org/10.1787/9789264268104-en.

In the **issue identification stage**, citizens can be involved to help identify the most pressing problems to solve, map the real needs of the public, or gather inputs or ideas to tackle the problem.

- Agenda setting mechanisms can allow citizens to propose ideas, prioritise needs, and contribute with evidence to the identification of pressing issues.
- Public authorities can involve citizens in the issue identification stage by:
    - Allowing citizens to raise awareness about pressing issues through digital platforms or petitions mechanisms.
    - Sharing the agenda setting with citizens through permanent or ad hoc mechanisms such as representative deliberative processes or citizen initiatives.

During the **policy or project formulation stage**, citizens can be involved to enrich a proposed solution, identify risks, prototype or test solutions, or collaboratively draft a policy, project plan, or legislation.

- Public authorities can involve citizens in the formulation stage by:
    - Establishing digital platforms and/or in-person mechanisms to allow citizens to comment, edit, or suggest changes to draft legislations or policy documents.
    - Creating spaces for citizens to participate in the design of solutions through, for example, workshops, feedback sessions, etc.

In the **decision-making stage**, citizens can be involved to collectively decide on the solution to be implemented, the budget to be allocated, or the projects that will be selected.

- Public authorities can involve citizens in the decision-making stage by:
    - Developing voting mechanisms (online or in-person) for citizens to express their preferences for suggested solutions or projects.
    - Giving citizens the final decision on the allocation of public resources through participatory budgets.

During the **implementation stage,** citizens can provide help in deploying the solutions or projects decided in the previous stage.

- Co-production is an overarching term to describe how public authorities can harness the skills, capabilities, and energy of citizens and stakeholders to deliver services that best meet the needs of future users.
- Public authorities can include citizens in the implementation phase by:
    - Engaging citizens in the creation of solutions or prototypes for services or projects, through hackathons, collaborative workshops, or maker spaces.
    - Creating spaces for co-creation between public authorities, citizens, and stakeholders as a way to continuously involve them in the implementation of projects or services. For example, open innovation labs, open spaces, recurrent public meetings, etc.

In the **evaluation stage**, citizens can be engaged to evaluate or monitor the implementation of the solution and to measure its outcomes and results.

- Public authorities can include citizens in the evaluation phase by:
    - Providing information and data about the policy, legislation, or project in question: the expected outcomes, the implementation progress, and the results. For example, through open data platforms, communication campaigns, open meetings, websites, etc.
    - Soliciting citizen feedback on services or projects implemented to support efficiency and improve results. Various methodologies can gather citizens' opinions and perceptions, such as polls, surveys, or Community Score Cards.

> Box 2.1. Questions to answer when defining the problem to solve and the moment of participation
>
> - What problem do you need to solve?
> - Where in the decision-making or policy cycle are you?
> - How can citizens and/or stakeholders help you solve this problem?

Step 2: Defining the expected objectives and results

Before involving citizens, it is essential to have a clear understanding of the objectives or expected results of the process. This will enable clarification about the desired inputs or contributions from citizens and the impact they will have on the final decision. This step will also help to identify the right public to involve (p26) and choose the right participation method (p30). It is very important to set clear expectations on the results of the process.

Expected objectives, and desired type of inputs

Inputs and contributions gathered through a participatory process can vary from broad ideas about a policy question, experts' opinions on the feasibility of a project, feedback on an existing proposal, or informed recommendations to solve a defined problem. The selected participation method and the design of the process will depend on the expected type of inputs or contributions from citizens, as not all methodologies allow for the same results.

In addition, the public needs to understand the future outcome of their contribution. This manages citizens' expectations and enhances their trust in the process and its result. Public authorities should decide and communicate in advance how they plan to use inputs received from the public during a participatory process and the impact they will have on the final decision. The expected outcome of the inputs gathered though a participatory process can vary from informative purposes (information) or a consultative exercise (consultation), to more impactful outcomes, potentially with binding results (engagement).

Table 2.1. Types of inputs or contributions from citizens and the expected impact on public decisions

Expected objectives of the participatory process	Examples of inputs gathered through a participatory process	Suggested methodology
Tap into the collective intelligence of the public to get ideas and inspiration that will help public authorities develop a plan for improving cycling infrastructure (**Consultation**)	**Ideas and proposals** to improve the cycling infrastructure in a metropolitan area	Public consultation Crowdsourcing Open Meeting
Test the proposal and gather insights from the public to adapt or enrich the proposal accordingly (**Consultation**)	Feedback and broad **opinions** on a draft roadmap or project proposal	Public consultation Open Meeting
Inform decision makers and adapt the original idea or solution based on the advice received (**Consultation**)	**Expertise or technical advice** on the use of European funds to support small and mid-size enterprises (SMEs)	Public consultation

Integrate the recommendations to suggested legislative amendments or policy documents (**Engagement**)	**Informed recommendations** on policy changes needed to ensure gender equality in the workplace	Representative deliberative process
Partner with participants to co-create solutions (**Engagement**)	**Concrete actions** such as prototypes of digital apps to measure the quality of air in an industrial area	Open innovation (hackathons or co-creation workshops)
Allow citizens to monitor the quality of public services or to inform about wrongdoings (**Consultation**)	**Feedback or alerts** on the quality of public services or the use of public funds	Civic monitoring
Give citizens and stakeholders the possibility to decide on the use of public resources through a participatory budget (**Engagement**)	**Decision** on how to distribute public resources for a specific purpose	Participatory Budget
Involve citizens in collecting data, information or evidence on water quality in urban areas (**Consultation**)	**Evidence** to inform a policy or a decision or to fill gaps in research	Citizen science
Identify a way forward that does not cause strong opposition from any social groups and gain legitimacy and support to implement it (**Engagement**)	**Broad consensus** of different social groups on a contentious issue	Representative deliberative process

Source: Author's own elaboration based on GovLab (2019) CrowdLaw Catalog Taxonomy, https://catalog.crowd.law/about.html#catalog

> **Box 2.2. Questions to answer whilst defining the desired inputs and expected outputs:**
>
> - What is the objective of involving citizens and or stakeholders?
> - What type(s) of inputs or contributions would you like to receive from participants?
> - How will you use these inputs to solve your problem?

Step 3: Identifying the relevant group of people to involve and recruiting participants

The next step is identifying the relevant group of people to involve. This decision will affect how the public will be recruited and can help define the participatory method. Different types of groups can be involved in a process, such as:

- Citizens (a broad, non-representative group);
- Citizens (a representative sample of a community);
- Citizens of a specific geographical area;
- Citizens of a sectoral group (youth, elderly, students, indigenous communities, etc.);
- Stakeholders such as NGOs, unions, universities, grassroots movements, businesses, etc.

In all of the above-mentioned cases, it is important to reach to participants from diverse backgrounds to increase inclusion and representation in the outcomes of the process. Defining the expected input (see p25) can help identify the relevant public to be involved, the type of recruitment, and the method of participation (see Table 2.2).

It is important to keep in mind that to address a specific policy issue there might be a need to engage with several types of groups that require different conditions and methods to participate. For example, for an infrastructure project, information meetings could be organised for inhabitants of the neighbourhood where the project will be built, in addition to roundtables with urbanists and accessibility experts, and a broader city-wide process to grasp public opinion. Such circumstances call for a participatory system, with separate processes planned in a sequential way, and where inputs received from one process feed into the one that follows.

Table 2.2. Examples of identifying the target public and choosing recruitment type

Expected input	Target public	Type of recruitment	Example of participatory process
Informed recommendations on legislative changes needed to ensure gender equality in the workplace	A representative sample of citizens	Civic lottery	**Citizens' Assembly** on Gender Equality
Prototypes of digital apps to measure the air quality in a former industrial area	A group of citizens with specific skills	Closed call	**Citizen science project** and a **hackathon** on air quality
Public opinion on the use of European funds	All interested or affected parties	Open call	**Public consultation** (opinion poll and surveys) to prioritise European funds
Diversity of stakeholder **views and opinions** about one topic or issue	Stakeholders representing diverse opinions	Closed call	**Public consultation** (dialogue roundtables) with civil society organisations
Ideas and proposals to improve the cycling infrastructure in a metropolitan area	Residents of a specific area	Open call	**A crowdsourcing platform** for citizens to suggest ideas on cycle paths
Feedback and broad opinion on a draft roadmap or project proposal	Broader public	Open call	**Public consultation** on an infrastructure project

Source: Author's own elaboration.

How to recruit participants?

There are different possible strategies for recruiting participants depending on the expected inputs, the targeted public, and the participation method. Prior to recruiting participants, a mapping exercise can be useful to identify relevant groups of citizens (for example, those affected by the problem to solve) or categories of stakeholders (for example, civil society organisations, businesses, groups of experts etc.) that hold the most relevant experiences, points of view, or expertise. It can also help minimise some of the open call risks described in this section.

Open call

In many traditional participatory processes, such as public consultations, there is often an "open call" to recruit participants, either to an in-person meeting or to participate in an online consultation or forum. Participation is usually encouraged by advertising the opportunity through different channels (online, social media, post, posters). Participation is open, so anyone who wants to is able to come in person or contribute online. In certain occasions, registration is open to anyone, but participants may be chosen through an application or selection process, depending on a criteria priorily defined (and communicated). Recruitment via "open call" aims to involve as many people as possible, however, there is a wealth of research that demonstrates that certain demographics tend to disproportionately participate, notably those who are older, male, well-educated, affluent, white, and urban (Dalton, 2008[6]; Kuser Olsen, Galloway and Ruth, 2018[7]; Smith, Lehman Schlozman and Verba, 2009[8]).

Closed call

Public authorities may also conduct consultations through a "closed call" for participants, meaning that politicians and/or civil servants might choose specific members of a community who have a particular expertise or experience needed to address a policy issue. In these instances, participation could be based on merit, experience, affiliation with an interest group, or because of their role in the community (see (MASS LBP, 2017[9]).

For example, a citizen science project aiming to improve air quality in classrooms might be interested in involving schools and will require a closed call and targeted recruitment of schools to take part in a project. Based on the target group, recruitment of participants can take place via organisations that represent these groups, going to places where members of the target group might be present or via tailored online communication campaigns that catch the attention of a desired audience.

Civic lottery

Civic lottery, or sortition, is used as a shorthand to refer to recruitment processes that involve random sampling from which a representative selection is made to ensure that the group broadly matches the demographic profile of the community (based on census or other similar data) (OECD, 2020[10]).

A civic lottery attempts to overcome the shortcomings and distortions of "open" and "closed" calls for participation described earlier. It ensures that nearly every person has an equal chance of being invited to participate in a participation process and that the final group is a microcosm of society. The golden standard is two-stage random selection. During the first stage, 2.000-30.000 invitations are sent out to a random sample of the population from the convening public authority. From those who respond positively, a second invitation to participate is sent out, stratified based on criteria such as age, gender, location, socio-economic criteria, and language (depending on the context). Invitations are usually signed by a figure of authority – for example, the mayor.

Figure 2.3. How to run a civic lottery?

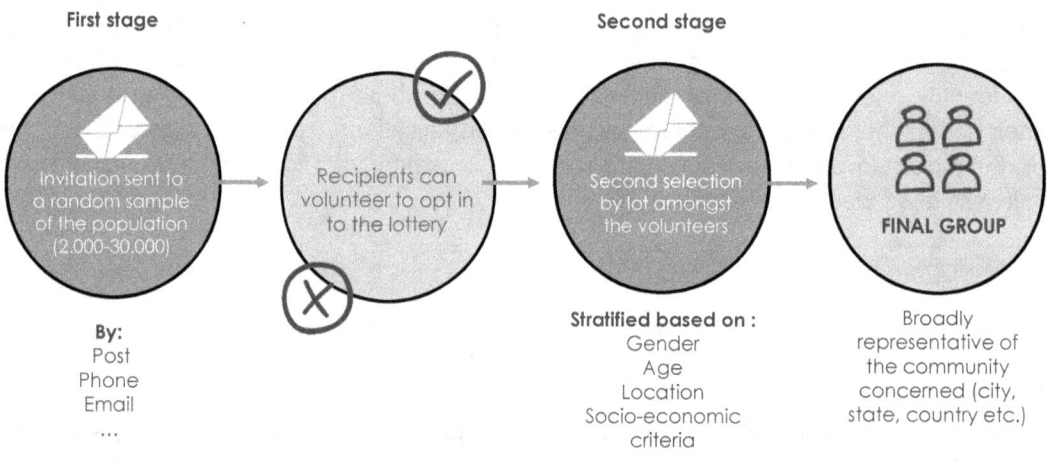

Source: Author's own elaboration based on OECD (2020) Innovative Citizen Participation and New Democratic Institutions: Catching the Deliberative Wave

A civic lottery is most often used when organising a representative deliberative process. Although it is not its exclusive use. A group of citizens selected via a civic lottery can also be convened for a participatory budget or a public consultation – in any circumstance when a participatory process requires maximum representativeness.

Recruiting participants via civic lotteries offers multiple benefits. Most importantly, the final group of participants is broadly representative of the wider public, which creates an opportunity to hear from a range of people with different lived experiences and opinions, in particular the usually underrepresented groups.

Some limitations of the civic lottery to keep in mind are its rather lengthy and expensive process, and limited breadth of participation.

How to motivate citizens to participate?

Beyond the careful design, planning, and implementation of a participatory process, public authorities also face the challenge of ensuring that citizens and stakeholders will be committed throughout the process. The main motivation to participate remains the commitment from organisers to use and integrate the received inputs in the final policy decision, so that they clearly see the impact of their time and effort. However, public authorities can reduce barriers and encourage inclusive participation through other design choices as well:

- **Providing financial compensation:** Public authorities can provide remuneration to participants to cover their expenses (transportation, childcare, food, digital tools, etc.) to ensure inclusiveness.
- **Providing a financial reward:** Citizens might receive an honorarium, a cash prize, public services vouchers, or other material benefits in exchange of their time and participation.
- **Providing childcare services:** For in-person processes, providing childcare facilities for children under a certain age can help break down the barriers of participation for people with children, particularly single parents.
- **Providing support to vulnerable groups**: To encourage inclusive and representative participation, public authorities can provide support to vulnerable groups such as disabled people or the elderly (such as accessible premises, sign language interpretation, etc.)
- **Making participation a social moment:** Citizens can be motivated to participate if this represents an opportunity to meet and interact with other members of their community (neighbours, co-workers, etc.) or with other citizens sharing their concerns. Participation can be part of a process to build a sense of belonging at the community level.
- **Offering recognition to citizens:** Citizen participation can be recognised as a civic virtue, as citizens are willing to give their time for a collective good. Public authorities can acknowledge citizens' efforts with diplomas, certificates, ceremonies, labels, etc.
- **Making participation fun and appealing:** Participatory processes can be inspired by gamification techniques to motivate citizens to get involved. The look, feel, and interface of digital tools used is also important to make the process appealing.
- **Making participation informative and interesting:** Citizens and stakeholders can learn from a participatory process (for example, about a policy area or how the government works). If citizens know that they will get new information or new skills, they might be more interested in participating.
- **Providing citizens with a questions & answers page when inviting their participation:** To citizens who do not typically participate in political or civic life, engaging in a consultation or participatory process can be daunting. Providing information about how the process will unfold, who will be there, and other information such as dress code can help ease people's fears and encourage those who are less inclined to participate for various reasons.

> Questions to answer throughout the identification of participants and their recruitment:
>
> - Given the task or problem to solve, what groups should be reflected among the participants? Who should be part of the process?
> - How many people should be involved?
> - How will participants be selected?
> - How to ensure – and maintain – the interest of participants throughout the process?

Step 4: Choosing the participation method

Once the problem to solve (see p22), the expected inputs (see p25), and the public you would like to involve (see p26) have been identified, it is time to choose the method of participation. There are many different methods that can be used to engage citizens in any given context, and new methods are continuously developed and implemented. These guidelines include eight different methods that are widely applied across public institutions, but acknowledge that there other methods that public authorities can use for their participatory processes.

The summary of methods detailed below compares their key characteristics.

Table 2.3. Citizen participation methods: Comparing key characteristics

Participation method	To use when you are looking for…	Considerations	Type of input it yields	Stage of decision-making process	Costs (on a scale from € to €€€)
ACCESS TO INFORMATION AND DATA Publishing information proactively and providing information reactively.	Ways to raise awareness about an issue or a public decision. Ways to keep the public informed about public decisions.	It is the very minimum that can be done. Should be used in situations where there is no room for citizens to have a say.	Promotes transparency, creates awareness about public issues, provides necessary information and creates conditions for more advanced methods of participation.	Identification Formulation Decision making Implementation Evaluation	Depending on the channels used to disseminate the information, but can usually be done with existing resources. €
OPEN MEETINGS / TOWN HALL MEETINGS Gathering the public in face-to-face meetings with public authorities, in order to provide information and openly discuss topics of interest.	Ways to inform the public about public issues and decisions. Space to have a loosely structured exchange and receive broad initial feedback. "Test the water" for initial reception of ideas and policies by the public.	Allows for an exchange between public authorities and the public. Does not yield representative judgement or well-informed solutions.	Information sharing and broad feedback from citizens.	Identification Formulation Decision making Implementation Evaluation	Depending on the scope, but can usually be done with existing resources. €
PUBLIC CONSULTATION	Aggregated individual opinions and feedback from the public.	Adaptable to the needs - can be done in a range of different methods, from	Aggregation of individual citizens' preferences or grouped opinions	Identification Formulation Decision	Depending on the method chosen and the scope of the consultation. It usually

A two-way relationship in which participants provide feedback to a public institution (such as comments, perceptions, information, advice, experiences, and ideas).	Opinions about a policy debate, or a specific question Experts' feedback.	surveys, digital platforms, to in-person discussions. Not statistically representative of the population Can be difficult to process the inputs received.	from stakeholders.	making	requires developing an adapted methodology or technical interface. If in person, participants will need a space and facilitators. € - €€
OPEN INNOVATION: CROWDSOURCING, HACKATHONS, AND PUBLIC CHALLENGES Tapping into the collective intelligence to co-create solutions to specific public problems via crowdsourcing, hackathons, or public challenges.	Ideas, and collective solutions to framed problems. Involve the public in developing solutions or prototypes.	Requires certain conditions and necessary resources for citizens and stakeholders to work on and develop solutions to public problems. Usually requires certain expertise from participants.	Collective ideation, co-creation of solutions, prototypes.	Identification Formulation Implementation Evaluation	Depending on the method chosen and the scope of the process. It usually requires a technical interface, some communication efforts, and a physical space for hackathons. € - €€
CITIZEN SCIENCE Involving citizens in one or many stages of a scientific (or evidence-based) investigation, including the identification of research questions, collection of data and evidence, conducting observations, analysing data, and using the resulting knowledge.	Help collecting or analysing scientific data. Feedback or guidance on research questions and research design. Collaboration to implement science related projects.	Is suited for scientific endeavours rather than policy questions and dilemmas. Adaptable to the needs – covers a range of participation opportunities in science.	Varies from data collected to guidance on research questions and decisions to implemented citizen projects.	Identification Implementation Evaluation	Depending on the method chosen and the scope of the process. It usually requires a technical interface, some communication efforts, could require a physical space for meetings, can require specific technical equipment (for example, air quality sensors to be made available for citizens for data collection purposes). € - €€€
CIVIC MONITORING Involving citizens in the monitoring and evaluation of public decisions, policies, and services. Civic monitoring can be considered as a social accountability mechanism.	Collaborative oversight and evaluation mechanisms for public decisions and actions. Ongoing monitoring of and feedback on a policy or a project. Community monitoring of a policy or a service.	It is an ongoing process which requires sustained participation. It is geared towards receiving feedback from individuals during or after implementation. It requires certain level of commitment from public authorities to take into account feedback to improve services or policies.	Citizen feedback, opinions, suggestions.	Implementation Evaluation	Depending on the method chosen, but it usually requires developing an adapted methodology or technical interface. € - €€
PARTICIPATORY BUDGETING Mechanisms that allow citizens and stakeholders to influence budgetary public decisions through the direct	Help from the public to identify budget or resource allocation preferences. Ideas and projects from the public to be funded. Increased awareness and understanding of	Creates conditions for the public to participate in decisions linked to public spending. Can yield either an aggregation of participants individual preferences (if takes	Varies from ideas, projects, prioritisation, to binding allocation of public resources through vote.	Identification Formulation Decision making Implementation	Depending on the scale and scope of the process. It usually requires intensive communication, human resources, developing an adapted methodology, and a technical interface.

allocation of public resources to priorities or projects or by being involved in public deliberations.	public spending by citizens.	the form of a voting), or their collective judgements (if it has a deliberative element).			€€ - €€€
REPRESENTATIVE DELIBERATIVE PROCESSES A randomly selected group of people who are broadly representative of a community spending significant time learning and collaborating through facilitated deliberation to form collective recommendations for policy makers.	Informed, collective public judgements about a complex policy issue. Recommendations that take into account a broad diversity of views. Legitimacy to take tough decisions.	Helpful when tackling complex, long-term policy issues. Can take place in different models ranging from shorter and smaller Citizens' Panels/Juries to larger scale, longer Citizens' Assemblies, or even permanent bodies.	Collective citizen recommendations, position, or judgement.	Identification Formulation Decision making Evaluation	Depending on the scale of the process. It usually requires intensive communication, human resources, an adapted methodology, a physical space to deliberate, skilled facilitation, and compensation for participants' time. €€ - €€€

Source: Author's own elaboration

ACCESS TO INFORMATION AND DATA

The first level of participation is information. Public authorities are usually obliged by legislation to publish a minimum set of public information and data both in a proactive and reactive manner (i.e. access to information or open data legislation). However, in these guidelines, information is seen both as a prerequisite for informed participation and as an enabler for more impactful levels of participation.

The OECD recognises the value of information and data for broader objectives such as trust, stronger democratic practices, and overall healthy civic spaces. The proactive disclosure of public information and data is understood as making available clear, complete, timely, reliable and relevant public sector data and information that is free of cost, available in an open and non-proprietary machine-readable format, easy to find, understand, use and reuse, and disseminated through a multi-channel approach, to be prioritised in consultation with stakeholders (OECD, 2017[11]).

- **Information and data as a prerequisite for informed participation:** public information and data can promote informed public debate and increase the quality of participatory processes. In this regard, public authorities can publish different types of information and data:
    - Legal framework and public information: constitution, laws, regulations, decrees, in different formats (text as well as machine readable) for all levels of government.
    - Policy making information: all the information needed to formulate policies like policy proposals, draft legislation, as well as speeches, press releases, benchmarks, external advice, impact assessments, audits, and policy reports.
    - Decision-making procedure, including agendas, actors involved, timeframe of debates and expected milestones to reach a decision, moments where the public can interact and influence the process, legal framework, stakeholders involved (especially interest groups), motives behind the final decision etc.
- **Information and data as an enabler for more impactful participation**: public information and data can empower citizens to understand and act upon the decisions that affect their lives, enable citizens to co-create solutions and support the effective monitoring of government actions.

- Public services information: Descriptions of services offered to the public, information on the recipients, guidance, booklets and leaflets, copies of forms, information on fees and deadlines. Governments should also publish the algorithms used for public service delivery when appropriate.
- Budget information: all budget related documents and data, projected budget, actual income and expenditure, and other financial information and audit reports. Governments should also publish the relevant formulas and algorithms when using projections and machine-based calculations.
- Implementation and evaluation, including information about the results of policies, annual reports, audits, and all necessary data and information to allow for public monitoring and evaluation.

In addition, public authorities should always provide the public with the possibility to request more information or provide feedback. For example, official websites could include dedicated sections or specific features (e.g., a contact box) for citizens to request further information or leave comments.

Box 2.3. Case studies: Access to information and data

Citizen Budget in Rwanda (2009-ongoing)

The Ministry of Finance and Economic Planning of Rwanda releases a citizen's guide to the national budget every fiscal year. This short booklet is available in English, Kinyarwanda, and French. It uses simple language and visual aids to convey the government's priorities and allocation of resources. It also includes general feedback on the suggestions made by citizens during the planning process through citizens' dialogues and platforms. Also known as Citizen Budgets, it is an information mechanism used in many other countries, such as Ghana, New Zealand, El Salvador, and South Africa.

More information can be found at: https://www.eprnrwanda.org/IMG/pdf/presentation_on_citizen_guide-2.pdf

Budget Monitor Portal for Public Engagement in Georgia

The Budget Monitor, an analytical portal managed by the State Audit Office of Georgia (SAOG), promotes transparency and public scrutiny of state finances. It provides sophisticated budgetary information through easy-to-interpret visualizations and dynamic graphs for free. Additionally, it enables citizens to get directly involved in the audit process by informing SAOG about corruption risks and wrongdoings in public organizations, expressing their interest in auditing particular agencies, or offering potential improvements in existing policies via alternatively designed policies that could be reflected in SAOG's recommendations. The system also provides information to the citizens about the results of their requests/petitions.

More information can be found at: https://budgetmonitor.ge/en

Open Justice Data from Criminal Court No 10 of Buenos Aires

Criminal Court No 10 of the city of Buenos Aires, Argentina, utilises digital tools to promote an open justice system. They collect, publish, and share all of their rulings and decisions on social media. In addition, they also have an open data repository and an open code dashboard with visual representations of the data collected.

More information can be found at: https://medium.com/participo/digital-tools-to-open-the-judiciary-a-perspective-from-argentina-e4bdcf56132

Open Contracting Dashboard of Colombia

The Open Contracting Dashboard (*Tablero de Contrataciones Abiertas de Colombia*) hosted by the national agency of procurements, Colombia Compra Eficiente (CCE), was designed based on user needs across the country to improve data visualization using CCE's data. This facilitates work by CSOs, investigative journalists, academia, private sector businesses, and public entities, enabling the visualization of more than 10 million procurement processes. It promotes access and understanding of public procurement data while identifying improvements and encouraging citizen participation.

More information can be found at: https://www.open-contracting.org/resources/best-practices-open-contracting-portals/

OPEN MEETINGS / TOWN HALL MEETINGS

What are open meetings and town hall meetings?

Open meetings and town hall meetings are participatory tools that can be traced all the way back to 17th-century New England meetings or colonial traditions in Latin America (*cabildos*). Nowadays, these processes are used worldwide, most often at local or legislative level, to foster information about public action, encourage citizen participation, and to build a relationship based on accountability and trust.

Characteristics

Open meetings and town hall meetings aim to gather the public in face-to-face meetings with public authorities, to provide information and openly discuss topics of interest chosen beforehand, contrary to public consultations, which aim specifically to gather citizens' inputs on a particular topic. These processes are based on dialogue and debate rather than deliberation (OECD, 2020[10]), and are more often used for information or consultation without a specific impact in the final decision.

Its main objectives are to inform citizens about public authorities' decisions and discuss them, to get citizens closer to public decision making, and to increase public transparency. Open meetings and town hall meetings can be complemented with other participatory methods. For example, a participatory budget can be supported by open meetings to present the process, enhance participation, and share the results.

Usually, these meetings are open to any resident the area to participate or to the broader public without geographical criteria. However, they are usually not designed to be particularly inclusive: limited and often traditional means of communication are used (street posters, for instance), therefore engaging already-interested citizens rather than pursuing representative or inclusive participation.

Town hall or open meetings are usually organised by public authorities at the local level, to support information sharing and discussions about day-to-day topics. However, these meetings can be organized at other levels of government, including the national or legislative levels.

For more information on how to design and implement an open meeting or a town hall meeting, please refer to **Chapter 4**.

> **Box 2.4. Case studies: Open meetings and town hall meetings**
>
> **Abuja Town Hall Meetings (Nigeria)**
>
> In 2003, the regional administration of Abuja, Nigeria, organised regular quarterly town hall meetings with residents of all six of its districts in order to get citizen feedback on infrastructure initiatives that were proving to be conflictive. The town hall meetings gathered thousands and were broadcast live on radio and later on television. The meetings were documented, and their results were integrated as action points by the Federal Capital Territory's Executive Committee. The practice remains to this day.
>
> More information can be found at: https://participedia.net/case/1148
>
> **Grand Débat National local meetings (France)**
>
> The French government organized the "Grand Débat National" in response to the "Yellow vests" protests. From January to April 2019, French citizens all over the country were invited to discuss and give their opinions on taxation and public spending, state organization of public services, the environment, and democracy and citizenship. Participation took place through various methodologies, one of which was in-person town hall meetings organised by local councils. During this period, more than 10.000 of these meetings took place.
>
> More information can be found at: https://granddebat.fr/
>
> **Citizen meetings for public infrastructure projects in Kadaň (Czech Republic)**
>
> Starting in 2017, the city of Kadaň instituted a policy of citizen meetings before public works decisions, e.g., before restoration of housing estates, traffic signs, or public greenery. The designer of the project presents their initial design and explains it to the public, who can then make comments and suggestions. If the designer deems that those suggestions are beneficial and feasible, they are incorporated, and a new version of the project is presented. Only then does the city undertake a public procurement process for the project. The city's website then publishes the minutes from the meetings.
>
> More information can be found at: http://kvalitavs.cz/wp-content/uploads/2018/06/Publikace_prikladu_dobre_praxe_-_Privetivy_urad_obci_III_typu_2018.pdf

PUBLIC CONSULTATION

What is a public consultation?

A consultation is a two-way relationship in which citizens provide feedback to a public institution (such as comments, perceptions, information, advice, experiences, and ideas). Usually, governments define the issues for consultation, set the questions, and manage the process, while citizens are invited to contribute their views and opinions (OECD, 2016[5]).

Characteristics

Public consultations are used to either gather ideas, feedback, inputs or opinions about a regulation, a policy question, or a draft proposal (legislation, strategy, etc.). A consultation can help design and shape decisions, or to identify ways that an already defined solution or policy can be improved.

Public consultations can be used to involve both citizens and/or stakeholders. When involving stakeholders (such as NGOs), public authorities can send targeted invitations, but when public consultations are open to the broader public, organisers need to prepare a robust communication strategy to ensure high levels of participation and to reach a diverse range of participants.

Public consultations can be done in many different ways, either in-person, online, or hybrid. The most common types are listed below.

Table 2.4. Types of public consultations

Type of public consultation mechanism	Description
Comment periods	Citizens and stakeholders are invited to submit their ideas to help solve a public problem or provide their feedback on a proposed policy. These are open to all and simple to set up online, however, they work better if there are roundtable discussions or other types of consultations set up in addition to it, where ideas can be developed and discussed. Comment periods favour participation of established stakeholders and actors over citizens, as they require time and resources to prepare ideas and suggestions to be submitted, which everyday citizens do not necessarily have.
Focus groups	A consultation tool used to determine peoples' preferences or to evaluate proposals and ideas. Usually, they involve a group of citizens who are testing or experiencing services, products or solutions and are asked to provide their in-depth feedback. They are usually comprised of around eight to ten people, gathered for a day or less.
Surveys	Help identify individual citizens' opinions and preferences based on a series of questions posed to citizens by governments. They can take place online or in person (e.g., to reach groups that do not have easy internet access). Surveys are often open to any respondent and hence are not representative.
Public opinion polls	Established instruments for portraying opinions held by a population on a given issue at a certain moment in time. They are a useful tool to gather the opinions of a random sample of the public, which ensures the statistical representativeness of their responses.
Workshops Seminars Conferences Round-table discussions	Used to gather more detailed stakeholder or expert opinions and create opportunities for exchange of ideas. They happen online or in person and involve around 20 to 150 participants. It is important to keep in mind that smaller group discussions are better suited for developing ideas and exchanging opinions, whereas bigger events can help frame the debate and raise awareness about the policy issue.
Interviews	Individual conversations with experts and stakeholders to gather their feedback and opinion regarding a project element, policy solution, or a service. They can be structured (a list of predetermined questions are asked), semi-structured (a few prepared questions and a further natural development of the conversation), or unstructured (starts with an open question and develops further based on the answer).

Source: Author's own elaboration based on OECD (2001), Citizens as Partners: OECD Handbook on Information, Consultation and Public Participation in Policy-Making ; and CitizenLab (2019), FAQ on digital consultation, https://www.citizenlab.co/ebooks-en/the-faqs-of-digital-consultation

For more information on how to design and implement a public consultation, please refer to **Chapter 4.**

Box 2.5. Case studies: Public consultations

Consultation to revamp the SP156 public services online portal (2018-2019)

In 2018, the São Paulo city council in Brazil conducted a public consultation in order to revamp its SP156 public services online platform, which had received complaints from citizens as being hard to use and employing a complicated language. City council officials invited users to give their feedback about the platform. They then collaborated on possible fixes, later presented as prototypes that users could test and comment on. About 320 people participated in the consultation, the result of which was a new platform with a 30% decrease in users' attrition rate.

More information can be found at: https://sp156.prefeitura.sp.gov.br/portal/servicos

> **Participatory constitution-making process of Chile**
>
> In 2015, Chilean President Michelle Bachelet announced a multi-stage process to draft a new constitution. The process was organised in three main stages. First, an online individual questionnaire gathered 90 804 responses. Next, there were local self-convened meetings of 10 to 30 people, taking place mostly in private spaces but also in universities, schools, churches, and other social spaces. Finally, more institutionalised participation took place through local cabildos or town hall meetings at the provincial and regional level. A parallel consultation was held for indigenous populations (6 478 participants) to include their voices in the new constitution. As per official numbers, 204 000 people participated in local meetings and 17 000 in the parallel indigenous consultation. The initial commitment of the Government was to send to Congress a new draft constitution, based on the Citizen Bases and then ratified through a plebiscite. A similar process was developed by Mexico City (Mexico) to collaboratively draft its Constitution. Using several types of consultation methods (surveys, polls, in-person questionnaires, roundtables, and a digital platform), the authorities gathered the opinion of thousands of inhabitants across the city.
>
> More information can be found at: http://redconstituyente.cl/wp-content/uploads/2018/04/An-assessment-of-the-Chilean-constituent-process-web.pdf
>
> **Comprehensive Consultations on Europe (Latvia 2018)**
>
> Almost 900 people took part in 23 events all around Latvia in order to gather feedback about the hopes, expectations, and fears of citizens regarding the future of the European Union. Half of these events were organised in tandem with CSOs, who were free to choose the format of the meetings. As a result, some were traditional discussions with experts, whereas others were workshops or brainstorms. In parallel to the in-person events, the Dialogi par Eiropas Nākotni crowdsourcing online platform gave citizens a chance to propose and vote on ideas, where more than 700 registered users contributed. Two Latvian CSOs produced a report summarising the ideas collected, which was then presented to Parliament.
>
> More information can be found at: https://oecd-opsi.org/innovations/comprehensive-consultations-on-europe/

OPEN INNOVATION: CROWDSOURCING, HACKATHONS, AND PUBLIC CHALLENGES

What are open innovation practices?

Open innovation practices, such as crowdsourcing, hackathons, or public challenges, are a way for public authorities to tap into collective intelligence to co-create solutions for specific public issues. Open innovation is regularly inspired from business development strategies or technological development, and can be defined as "the cooperative creation of ideas and applications outside of the boundaries of any single organisation" (Seltzer and Mahmoudi, 2012[12]).

Characteristics

Open innovation methods are usually used to convene expertise from citizens and stakeholders to find ideas or inspiration, prototype and test solutions, or to improve services or methods (GovLab, 2019[13]).

- **Crowdsourcing** refers to the idea of using the expertise and ideas coming from the crowd (in this case broader citizens and stakeholders). It can be used to gather inputs throughout the policy-cycle of any public decision. Through digital platforms or in-person activities, public authorities can gather inputs from expert groups, targeted stakeholders (such as scientists or developers), or the wider public to answer specific public problems (GovLab, 2019[13]).
- **Hackathons** (from hack and marathons) are in-person or virtual events bringing together public authorities and stakeholders to collaboratively work on ideas, prototype solutions, and services to solve public problems. The idea is to take advantage of the diversity of skills, expertise, and profiles to find new approaches or innovative solutions. Usually, hackathons involve technical communities (developers, coders, designers, data scientists, etc.) to make use of data previously published (in an open data format) by the public authority convening the event. Hackathons are organised during a short period time (24 to 72 hours), where participants can work in sprint to solve a policy problem, design or code digital solutions such as dashboards, applications, websites, etc.
- **Public challenges** are co-creation mechanisms where citizens and stakeholders propose solutions to concrete public problems. The public authority publishes a specific problem or challenge, and then selects the best proposals coming from the public to solve the problem in question. Solutions can be policy proposals, prototypes of mobile applications, project suggestions, etc. Citizens and stakeholders submit their proposals, and, based on previously published criteria, the public authority selects the best ranked solutions. In some cases, the public authority provides a reward to the selected solutions (such as financial compensation, public recognition, or other awards). The public authority can then implement those solutions (as new public services, or as part of a wider policy program) or provide support for the participants to develop their project (as coaching sessions, financial resources, etc.).

There are different approaches regarding who can participate in open innovation methodologies such as crowdsourcing, hackathons, or public challenges.

- **Universal access:** the process is open to all interested citizens and stakeholders without requiring a specific skill, expertise, or profile.
- **Specific audiences**: some processes can be aimed at more targeted audiences or public with specific skills or expertise such as technical communities, scientists, designers, etc.

For more information on how to design and implement an open innovation process, to please refer to **Chapter 4.**

> **Box 2.6. Case studies: Open innovation**
>
> **Open Innovation practices at NASA**
>
> The National Aeronautics and Space Administration (NASA), based in Washington, D.C. frequently launches hackathons, crowdsourcing initiatives, and public challenges. These aim to gather solutions for issues as broad as advancing technology to adapt to life in outer space, establishing a long-term presence on the moon, and general problem-solving during the Covid-19 pandemic.
>
> For instance, NASA engaged the public with 56 public prize competitions and challenges, and 14 citizen science and crowdsourcing activities over 2019 and 2020. They awarded $2.2 million in prize money, with members of the public submitting over 11.000 solutions.
>
> More information can be found at: https://www.nasa.gov/solve/index.html
>
> **Mexico City Bus Routes Mapathon (2013)**
>
> To map a complex, large, and informal bus system, authorities in Mexico City organized a citywide participatory game. Players competed to win money and other prizes by downloading an app and earning points by riding buses while sharing their GPS data and feeding information about routes into the collaborative database with the goal of mapping the system. In total, 4,000 users covered more than 30.000 miles of public transport routes giving the government valuable information on bus routes, length of journeys, passage frequency, duration, and fares. This citizen-collected data allowed the authorities to create a database and inform policy-makers on future mobility policies and reforms.
>
> More information can be found at: https://nextcity.org/urbanist-news/big-data-mexico-city-mapathon-gamifies-crowdsourcing
>
> **Chinese Taipei Presidential Hackathon (2018-ongoing)**
>
> Starting in 2018, the Presidential Hackathon is an annually recurring initiative that aims to bring together data owners, data scientists, and field experts to find solutions to common issues with the help of technology and innovative ideas.
>
> More information can be found at: https://presidential-hackathon.taiwan.gov.tw/en/
>
> **France's hackathons on taxation and fiscal policies**
>
> The French Ministry of Finances organizes recurrent hackathons to improve their algorithms and applications. For example, in 2016, the Government published the taxation algorithm to allow for scrutiny and improvement, and for developers to create new services and applications. The culture of hackathons has expanded to all Ministries in France, and has been used for example, to collectively process the millions of inputs received via online platforms during the Grand Débat National.
>
> More information can be found at: https://www.etalab.gouv.fr/codeimpot-un-hackathon-autour-de-louverture-du-code-source-du-calculateur-impots/

CITIZEN SCIENCE

What is citizen science?

Citizen science has a long history, as amateur enthusiasts of science, astronomy, biology, and other sciences have been exploring and observing the world around them for thousands of years. With the advancement of online technologies, it has become much more prominent and efficient, and is now employed by researchers, advocates, and communities all over the world.

The essence of citizen science is that citizens are involved in one or many stages of a scientific investigation, like identifying research questions, conducting observations, analysing data, and using the resulting knowledge (Craglia and Granell, 2014[14]). It is a way to democratise a scientific process, opening it up to everyday people, and tapping into their motivation and curiosity to co-create and further research goals.

Characteristics

Citizen science methods can be used for several different purposes (Veeckman et al., 2019[15]):

- **As an opportunity for citizens to learn more about a specific field or issue.** Such objectives can be achieved by citizen science projects that open access to the results of scientific research to citizens for free (such as open access journals) or organising informal learning workshops. Such efforts would be considered as an initial step of citizen participation: information.

- **As a research approach, where citizens contribute by gathering or analysing data.** The key strength of recruiting citizen scientists to contribute to research by collecting and analysing data is the large amount of data citizens are able to collect, the diversity of the data (since citizens are dispersed across different geographical locations and it would be impossible to gather it otherwise), and the opportunity to process and analyse data on a larger scale. The data collection can be done via observation, such as counting a specific kind of bird in one's neighbourhood, or using technical devices, such as air quality meters. Such efforts would be considered as citizen consultation or engagement, depending on the mandate given to citizens.

- **As a method to give citizens a voice in shaping research questions, designing a project, determining a focus of a study.** Citizens can be valuable and active agents in shaping the research process for some projects. Their personal experience of living in a specific location, interacting with a specific environment, and being part of a particular community can yield important insights and helpful suggestions when identifying research questions or determining a focus of the study. In addition, involving citizens in the co-design of the research project contributes to raising awareness around the issue the study aims to analyse, and can further help influence policy decisions and demonstrate the importance of the issue. Such efforts would be considered as citizen consultation or engagement, depending on the mandate given to citizens.

Both everyday people and stakeholders can be involved in citizen science projects, depending on the purpose of the project and technical requirements. They usually play different roles: while citizens are at the heart of the process, stakeholders provide support, inputs, and access to data or tools.

For more information on how to design and implement a citizen science process, please refer to **Chapter 4.**

> **Box 2.7. Case studies: Citizen science**
>
> **Plastic Pirates**
>
> This campaign was started by the Portuguese, Slovenian, and German joint Trio-Presidency of the Council of the European Union for 2020 and 2021. It allows classrooms, teachers, and other associations to engage children by contributing to the study of pollution in European rivers.
>
> Project materials can be directly downloaded from the website and children can be brought to different river sections. They can then identify and classify different types of plastic pollution along the rivers. Their results are then added to an interactive digital map that can in turn be used by the scientific community to gradually close the gaps in the existing research on the amount of different types of plastic waste.
>
> More information can be found at: https://www.plastic-pirates.eu/en
>
> **Sensor.Community**
>
> Sensor.Community is a global network of environmental sensors that create open environmental data. Anyone can contribute directly by installing a DIY air quality or noise wherever they are. There are currently more than 14,000 sensors in 71 countries worldwide which all feed into an interactive digital map. The data produced by the network can then be used by the scientific community and health authorities in order to monitor air and noise pollution.
>
> More information can be found at: https://sensor.community/en/

CIVIC MONITORING

What is civic monitoring?

In the context of these guidelines, civic monitoring refers to the idea of involving the public in the monitoring and evaluation of public decisions, policies, and services. This participatory method can also be considered as a vertical or social accountability tool, as it allows citizens and stakeholders to directly participate in making public authorities accountable for their decisions or actions.

Characteristics

Public institutions can largely benefit from creating feedback channels for the public to provide inputs, comments, and complaints to improve the decisions, actions, and services provided. When involving citizens and stakeholders in the oversight and evaluation of its decisions and actions, public authorities can create virtuous circles and healthier relationships that can contribute to overall trust in government. Civic monitoring can allow the public to monitor key areas of government action, such as:

- **Budget**: Opening up budgets and public financial management and providing spaces for direct citizen participation to provide ongoing feedback and timely collaboration to receive inputs can reduce corruption and waste, and increase the odds of taxes being used to deliver quality public services and to achieve real improvements in living standards and in social, economic, and environmental outcomes (OECD, 2017[16]). In addition to being accountable in the collection of revenues, governments should also be accountable for the management and execution of the budget. Concretely, citizens and stakeholders can monitor and evaluate the budget by reviewing the information and data published by public institutions or ensuring that the money was indeed spent in the way it was intended.

- **Policies**: Civic monitoring in policy making is focused on the implementation and evaluation stages of the policy process. Concretely, it is about ensuring that policies achieve their expected outcome, benefit the desired publics, and are efficient vis-à-vis the public resources involved (GovLab, 2019[13]). The public can gather evidence and inform about the real outcomes of policies to be able to assess the policy impact in comparison to the expected results.
- **Public services:** Involving citizens and stakeholders in monitoring and evaluation can promote efficiency and improve access as well as quality of public services. Mechanisms to hold public services to account can focus on different aspects and at different stages of the service design and delivery process, such as:
    - **Spending**: how much is the government spending on which activities? Is the allocated budget in line with public preferences?
    - **Performance**: is the public service achieving its intended results? How are public authorities delivering public services? How are users perceiving and evaluating the performance of the public service?
    - **Access**: is the target public being correctly given access to these services? If the public service is intended to be universal, do all groups have equal access?

Civic monitoring can be done in different ways, whether in-person or using digital tools. The most common ones are listed below.

Table 2.5. Typology of civic monitoring mechanisms

	Description of mechanism
Public opinion surveys	Participatory surveys are powerful tools that seek citizen feedback on the quality and performance of public services such as primary and secondary education, healthcare, public transportation, and the water supply network. Surveys and report cards directly engage citizens in assessing the quality of public services in terms of quality, access, and availability. Governments can systematically gather this feedback, periodically publish the responses on their website, and then use this information to benchmark citizen satisfaction with public services over time.
Citizen Report Cards (CRC)	A citizen report card on public services is not just one more opinion poll. Report cards reflect the actual experience of people with a wide range of public services by soliciting user feedback on service provider performance. During a CRC process, quantitative and perception-based information from statistically representative surveys is gathered, which means that the findings reflect the opinions and perceptions of the citizen group from which input and information is being sought. As such, it is a useful tool for establishing sound baseline information and benchmarking service coverage and performance, as well as identifying inequities in service delivery.
Social audits	Mechanism to keep the community informed about government services and allow citizens to hold them to account. These audits are formal reviews of the objectives, decision making processes, and public resources in public institutions. Social audit processes can help focus on government performance and/or behaviour, denounce corrupt practices, or disseminate information about a public officials' asset declaration before an election. Social audit activities can take place at any stage of the policy making cycle and can help measure public policy consistency between expected and actual outcomes.
Citizen complaint mechanisms	Citizen complaint mechanisms allow citizens to submit complaints about a public service, an action performed by a public servant or the overall perception of a public institution. These mechanisms can often be lodged on-site or in public hearings, although most institutions also offer various channels, such as hotlines, mailboxes, and online submission forms to enable diversity and accessibility. Registering complaints is the most common way through which any citizen can alert about possible fraud, corruption or mismanagement of public funds, or alleged irregularities within state agencies or government programs.
Community-based monitoring and evaluation	Monitoring and evaluation activities describe the collection and assessment of measurable outputs from projects being planned and implemented in communities in order to measure their success and analyse their impact. Community-based monitoring and evaluation is key to ensuring that citizens with expertise as well as experience of the public services in their area are involved in the policymaking process and the outcomes of projects.
Public Expenditure Tracking (PET)	Public expenditure tracking involves tracing the flow of public resources for the provision of public goods or services from origin to destination (CIVICUS, 2014). It is a mechanism for citizens and civil society to be involved in monitoring the use of public resources and for public authorities to increase efficiency and decrease corruption or misuse.
Online tools	Citizens can also monitor public action and report to a wider community through the use of apps, virtual forums, social media or dedicated websites. It is more and more common that citizens take on social media to complain about the degradation of a public space, or to evaluate publicly their experience when using a public service (in a positive or negative way). More and more local governments are also putting in place dedicated mobile applications or digital

	solutions to allow the public to alert when a public service is malfunctioning (such as the public transport system) or when the streets are not clean, the public lighting is not working, etc.
Representative deliberative processes	During these processes, randomly selected citizens, comprising a microcosm of a community, spend significant time learning and collaborating through facilitated deliberation to develop informed collective recommendations for public authorities. Public authorities are obliged to publicize all relevant information about the policy issue or the service and report back on recommendations made by citizens. This type of processes can be used for citizens to evaluate a public service or a public policy by providing recommendations on how to improve its delivery or implementation. Standing panels can also be set up to monitor a certain policy or project over time.

Source: Author's own elaboration based on OECD (2020), Handbook on Open Government for Peruvian Public Servants, https://www.oecd.org/gov/open-government/guia-de-la-ocde-sobre-gobierno-abierto-para-funcionarios-publicos-peruanos.htm

There are different approaches regarding who can participate in civic monitoring mechanisms.

- **Universal access**: the process is open to all interested citizens and stakeholders without requiring a specific skill, expertise, or profile.
- **Specific audiences**: some mechanisms can be aimed at more targeted audiences or public with specific skills or expertise such as technical communities, scientists, designers, etc. It can also target users of specific public services, or residents of limited geographical areas, etc.

For more information on how to design and implement a civic monitoring process, please refer to **Chapter 4.**

> **Box 2.8. Case studies: Civic monitoring**
>
> **Citizen Report Card on Public Services in Bangalore**
>
> The Citizen Report Card methodology was developed in Bangalore, India in the 1990s. The first exercise took place in 1993, when more than 800 households were surveyed on their satisfaction with public service providers. The survey questions asked respondents to rate public services on different scales, which were then aggregated to provide the "grade" for each government agency. The results were shared with public officials and widely publicised. The exercise was then repeated in 1999 and 2003, with significant improvement shown in the latter instance. CRC exercises have also been implemented in places such as California, Vietnam, and Ukraine.
>
> More information can be found at: https://www.internationalbudget.org/wp-content/uploads/Public-Affairs-Centre-Develops-Citizen-Report-Cards-in-India.pdf
>
> **Marea Digital**
>
> Marea Digital is a civic tech platform that allows citizens of Buenaventura, Colombia to identify and report local issues affecting the community, as well as promote local initiatives that are working for the welfare of the residents.
>
> The platform has a map and geo-referencing for each of the communes of Buenaventura, users can access it and report problems or community initiatives around five thematic areas: gender, education, infrastructure, health, and COVID-19. From there, a report status is generated (with open data). Citizens can then start a dialogue with the institution that can result in - depending on the case - the reception, processing, and solution of the report.
>
> More information can be found at: https://www.mareadigital.org/
>
> **Promise Tracker**
>
> Promise Tracker is a collaborative data collection platform that allows citizens to define an issue they would like to tackle and then collect data about it to be shared with decision makers. Citizens can create simple data collection forms for civic monitoring campaigns. All data collected can be viewed in maps and simple graphics as part of the dedicated web page for each campaign. In addition, it guides users through raising awareness on the topic and defining the problem, to identifying the key actors to engage, in order to develop solutions. It has thus far been for various campaigns in Brazil.
>
> More information can be found at: https://promisetracker.org/en/

PARTICIPATORY BUDGETING

What is participatory budgeting?

Participatory budgeting is a democratic way for people to have a direct say on how public money is spent. It began in 1989 in Porto Alegre in southern Brazil. In Brazil alone, this participatory mechanism spread to more than 436 municipalities, and today we can count more than 11,000 participatory budgeting experiences around the world (Participatory Budgeting Atlas, 2021[17]).

Characteristics

A participatory budget refers to mechanisms that allow citizens and stakeholders to influence public decisions through the direct allocation of public resources to priorities or projects. The Participatory Budgeting World Atlas (2021[17]) defines a participatory budget as a "process that involves a specific portion or the entire amount of an institution's budget, so that can be freely and independently decided by all the citizens participating in the initiative". These guidelines identify two types of participatory budgets:

- **Project-based processes:** a pre-defined amount of the budget is allocated to citizens' projects and ideas. The amount depends on each authority, and it can go up to 100 million euros per year as in Paris (France), where the biggest amount of budget is put up to citizen vote (Véron, 2016[18]).
- **Budget cycle processes**: citizens and stakeholders can participate throughout the budget cycle, by providing comments or making recommendations on the overall budget or strategical priorities. This can be done by creating a dedicated participatory body or by inviting participants to public decisions bodies such as budget committees.

The majority of processes are organized by local governments; however, it is important to take into consideration those experiences organized by other levels of government such as regional, state, and national. For example, Portugal, where a national participatory budget is in place as of April 2021 (see Box 2.9).

There are different approaches regarding who can take part in a participatory budget:

- **Universal access:** the process is open to all individuals of a certain territory or institution.
- **Targeted audiences**: some processes can be aimed at more targeted audiences or specific social sectors such as young people, residents of a specific area, the elderly, immigrants, women, LGBTQI communities, etc.

The goal of a participatory budget should be to make fiscal public decisions more open, meaning more transparent, accountable, and participatory. It helps citizens to better understand the functioning of public budgeting, influence spending priorities, and increase budget and fiscal accountability (OECD, 2007[19]).

For more information on how to design and implement a participatory budget, please refer to please refer to **Chapter 4.**

> **Box 2.9. Case studies: Participatory budgeting**
>
> **Kotrijk Participatory Budgeting (2021)**
>
> The participatory budgeting process of the city of Kotrijk in Belgium incorporates elements of deliberation in conjunction with the traditional PB methods. Citizens can propose their ideas online, after which a randomly selected citizen jury deliberates and recommends certain proposals for their neighbourhoods. Then they move on to budget gaming. Here, citizens can negotiate with each other about (fictive) budgets related to the proposals from the online platform. The output of these budget games become a source of input for the randomly selected citizen jury to make the final recommendations.
>
> More information can be found at: https://www.kortrijk.be/burgerbudget
>
> **School Participatory Budgeting (2017)**
>
> After several schools decided to experiment with school participatory budgeting, in 2017, Phoenix's Union High School District (USA) implemented this concept on a larger scale, introducing a district-wide opportunity for participatory budgeting. Students brainstormed ideas for school improvement projects for six months, after which they developed formal plans which were then put to a school-wide vote.
>
> More information can be found at: https://www.pxu.org/PB
>
> **Portugal national Participatory Budgeting**
>
> The Portugal Participatory Budget (PPB) is the first participatory budget done at the country level. To ensure the maximum engagement of citizens from all over the country, the PPB consists of a hybrid participatory model that combines digital and face-to-face interactions. The face-to-face approach is mainly based on participatory meetings held nationwide, in which the population is able to present and discuss their ideas in person, with the assistance of facilitators. In addition, citizens can also submit their proposals at the Citizens Spots (assisted digital services counters) and at some public libraries all around the country. The citizens can use digital tools to participate, but also more traditional channels, so anyone can take part of the initiative, even the ones with fewer digital skills or without internet access.
>
> More information can be found at: https://oecd-opsi.org/innovations/portugal-participatory-budget/
>
> **Citizen Budget Committee in Oregon (United States)**
>
> The Budget Committee is made up of five county commissioners and five citizens. This committee reviews and approves the County budget, limits the amount of tax which may be levied by the County and establishes a tentative maximum amount for total permissible expenditures for each department and fund in the County budget.
>
> More information can be found at:
> https://lanecounty.org/government/county_departments/county_administration/administration/budget_and_financial_planning/citizen_involvement_opportunities

REPRESENTATIVE DELIBERATIVE PROCESSES

What is a representative deliberative process?

Representative deliberative process: a process in which a broadly representative body of people weighs evidence, deliberates to find common ground, and develops detailed recommendations on policy issues for public authorities (OECD, 2021[20]). Common examples of one-off processes are citizens' assemblies, juries, and panels. The use of these processes, named as a "deliberative wave", has been growing since the 1980s, gaining momentum since around 2010.

Figure 2.4. What is a representative deliberative process?

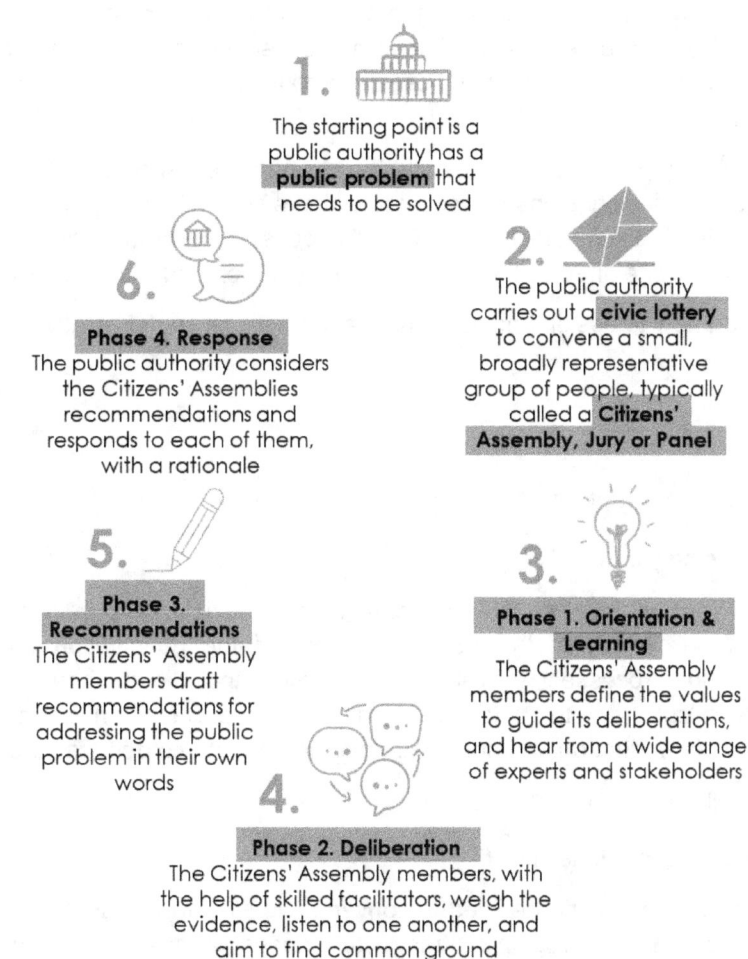

Source: Author's own elaboration based on OECD (2020) Innovative Citizen Participation and New Democratic Institutions: Catching the Deliberative Wave

Characteristics

A representative deliberative process is most suited to address the following types of problems:
- Values-based dilemmas;
- Complex problems that require trade-offs and affect a range of groups in different ways;
- Long-term questions that go beyond electoral cycles.

There are two elements that make representative deliberative processes quite different from other methods of citizen participation.

- **Random selection of participants through a civic lottery.** To be able to organise deep and substantial deliberation, the group of citizens participating in it must be relatively small, usually ranging from 15 to 100 participants. Randomly selecting citizens, stratified based on criteria such as age, gender, location, and socio-economic background, has the benefit of capturing the diversity of views, perspectives, and lived experiences of different members of society and ensuring broad representativeness of that community. Even though it is a smaller group of participants than some other participatory processes, it is designed to ensure inclusiveness and capture the views of those harder-to-reach communities and voices. See more details about this recruitment method in the Civic lottery section of these Guidelines.
- **Deliberation**. Deliberation involves dialogue and debate, but also implies a careful consideration of a range of different arguments and opinions in a respectful way. It requires accurate and relevant information and adequate time, so that those deliberating can go into the core of the issue and find common ground.

Overall, because of these properties, representative deliberative processes focus on the depth of deliberation and all parts of society being represented within a smaller group of participants, whereas the majority of other methods of citizen participation place the focus on the breadth of participation – aiming to ideally directly involve everyone affected by a specific issue (Carson and Elstub, 2019[21]; OECD, 2020[10]).

For more information on how to design and implement a representative deliberative process, please refer to **Chapter 4.**

Box 2.10. Case studies: Representative deliberative processes

The Irish Citizens' Assembly (2016-2018)

The Irish Citizens' Assembly involved 100 randomly selected citizen members who considered five important legal and policy issues: the 8th amendment of the constitution on abortion; ageing populations; referendum processes; fixed-term parliaments and climate change. The Assembly's recommendations were submitted to parliament for further debate. Based on its recommendations, the government called a referendum on amending the 8th amendment and declared a climate emergency.

More information can be found here: https://www.citizensassembly.ie/en/

Infrastructure Victoria Citizens' Juries (2016)

The regional government of Victoria decided to convene two simultaneous citizens' juries in order to deliberate on the questions of the region's infrastructure needs and ways to finance said projects. 43 randomly selected members (per jury) met in Melbourne and Shepparton for six non-consecutive days in order to discuss the question and deliver a 30-year plan acknowledging the citizenry's priorities. They provided 137 recommendations and the government had 12 months to deliver an official response.

More information can be found here: https://www.newdemocracy.com.au/2016/02/01/infrastructure-victoria-meeting-victoria-s-infrastructure-needs/

Citizens' Jury on the Construction of Gwangju Metropolitan Subway Line No. 2 (2018)

The city of Gwangju in South Korea convened a Citizens' Jury to deliberate on the construction of line 2 of their metropolitan subway system. The city council decided to go down that route after 16 years of internal conflict and political gridlock. 250 randomly selected citizens participated in an overnight public

> deliberation, along with other stakeholders. They recommended that the city should go ahead with the construction of the line, but making sure to implement other measures to prevent wasted resources and address other concerns.
>
> More information can be found here: https://en.kadr.or.kr/blank-4

Step 5: Choosing the right digital tools

Deciding if and how to use digital tools

The use of digital tools for citizen participation is a widespread practice at all levels of government around the world. It is normal for public authorities to be prone to reach out to the public using digital tools, as it might seem more accessible, easy to put in place, allowing for an instantaneous and massive participation, etc. However, the question about digital tools should only arise after the first four steps outlined above. It should not be the starting point when planning or designing a citizen participation process. There should first be clarity about the purpose, stage of the policy cycle, expected inputs and how they will be used, and the methodology. Only then is it relevant to ask if (and if yes, which) digital tools are the most appropriate. Moreover, before using digital tools for participatory processes, public authorities must take into account some considerations:

- **Keeping in mind the existing "digital divides":** Societies can be divided into people who do and people who do not have access to - and the capability to use - digital technologies. It is important to avoid the emergence of new forms of "digital exclusion" (i.e., not being able to take advantage of digital services and opportunities). For example, men, urban residents, and young people are more likely to be online than women, rural populations, and older persons (International Telecommunication Union, 2021[22]). When possible, digital tools should be implemented alongside in-person methods, to increase inclusion and bridge the digital divide.
- **Using digital tools requires resources:** Using digital tools does not imply that the costs or the needed resources will be reduced, so public authorities should not think about digital as a saving option. On the contrary, a qualitative use of digital tools, one that ensures inclusion and impactful participation requires technical, human, and financial resources. In some cases, public authorities might want to outsource (meaning contract external resources for a limited period) the set-up and management of digital tools. In other cases, they can use internal resources. It is important to avoid overlaps, so it is recommended that public authorities reach out to colleagues or dedicated offices in their institutions to ensure that a digital platform is not already in place or if a digital tool has been pre-selected by the institution for these types of uses.
- **The technological choice:** As it has become evident in the latest electoral campaigns, technology such as algorithms and social media can have a direct impact on the democratic process and the outcomes of a citizen participation process. Public authorities should think twice before selecting a digital tool, i.e. ensuring that the technology selected is transparent and accountable. These guidelines do not endorse any digital tool in particular, but evidence shows that open-source software is best suited for democratic processes because it allows for scrutiny, accountability, and collaboration.

Selecting the right tool

Digital tools can allow citizens and stakeholders to interact and submit their inputs in different ways:

- Being informed through data and visualisations;

- Proposing new projects, ideas, or suggestions;
- Deliberating to agree on shared decisions;
- Voting on suggested ideas or projects;
- Prioritising potential options;
- Drafting strategies, policies, or legislation collaboratively;
- Mind-mapping, interactive polling;
- Recognising patterns and trends in submitted responses, views, and opinions;
- Sharing information or data to fill an existing gap.

Selecting the right tool will depend on the citizen participation method used, the public to be involved, the expected output, the available resources, etc. People Powered has developed an interactive Guide to Digital Participation Platforms to support public authorities in selecting the right tool. It includes a matrix of the best digital tools for participation which **offers a quick overview of each platform's characteristics.**

The list of existing digital solutions is very extensive, and the objective is not to map all the possibilities in these guidelines. The table below presents a list of digital tools that can be used in the context of the methods presented in this document. All the tools listed are open source, which means that the public can see, replicate, and collaborate on the code. Nevertheless, public authorities can also decide to develop and design their own platform, adapted to their specific needs.

Table 2.6. Selecting the right digital tool for citizen participation

Tool	Open meeting	Public consultation	Crowdsourcing	Citizen Science	Civic monitoring	Participatory budget	Representative deliberative process
Your Priorities		X	X	X	X	X	
All Our Ideas		X	X	X			
Pol.Is		X	X				X
Decidim	X	X	X			X	X
DemocracyOS		X				X	
Jit.si	X						X
Consul	X	X	X			X	
HackMD FramaPad Etherpad	X			X			X
CitizenLab		X		X		X	
Virtual Congress		X	X				
Loomio		X	X	X	X		
Digital Consultations		X	X				
UnHangout	X	X					X
Discourse	X	X	X				

Source: Author's own elaboration.

The Inter-American Development Bank has put in place a repository of open-source tools that can be used in the context of participatory processes. These tools can be replicated by any interested authority and range from collaborative drafting, monitoring of commitments, public consultations, to citizen alerts.

> Box 2.11. Questions to answer when considering the use of (and setting up) digital tools for participation:
>
> - Are digital or online tools needed for your process?
> - What tools will you use?
> - How will you ensure that everyone has access and is able to use those tools?

Step 6: Communicating about the process

Quality communication is a prerequisite to organising a successful participatory process. It can help at every step of the way – from recruiting citizens, to ensuring transparency of the process, and extending the benefits of learning about specific policy issues to the broader public. As mentioned in the joint OECD-Open Government Partnership (OGP) *Guide on Communicating Open Government* (OECD and OGP, 2019[23]), such tools can highlight existing opportunities for individuals to contribute to laws, for example, or to widen the government's interactions with the public and target specific groups, including traditionally underrepresented ones (OECD, 2021[24]).

When communicating about any participatory process, it is helpful to:

- Distinguish between communication with the participants of the process and communication with the broader public about the participation process (see Table 2.7).
- Prepare a communications strategy and plan that follows every step of the process and is based on audience insights.
- Consider which channels are appropriate to reach your audience. Younger citizens might prefer online and social media, whereas older citizens might be more easily reached by post, print newspapers, or posters in local supermarkets.
- Ensure constant, clear, and understandable communication that does not use technical language. Unclear information in technical language can easily discourage any form of participation.
- Consider translating the communications into all the languages that are spoken by the communities addressed, this is important to ensure inclusion and to reach out to a broad public.

Table 2.7. How to communicate during a participatory process?

Communication with participants	Communication with the broader public
- **Purpose:** helpful at recruiting participants, keeping them engaged, and ensuring a smooth experience. - **Channels:** phone, email, a variety of social media outlets (such as a dedicated Facebook or WhatsApp group), or a dedicated online platform.	- **Purpose:** raising interest, understanding, and awareness about the participatory process and the issue it tackles, ensuring transparency and building trust in the decisions made by the participants. Explaining the selection of participants and how decisions were made can be key to the perceived legitimacy of a participation process. - **Channels:** ongoing communication on a dedicated website, making relevant information public, social

	media posts, videos, press releases, or press conferences.

Source: Author's own elaboration.

> **Box 2.12. Using plain language to communicate**
>
> Using plain language can support public institutions in simplifying technical policy messages and disseminating information on government activity more clearly. This type of communication centres the principle of accessibility by designing content for the average reader through simple vocabulary, short sentences, headings, key words, and visual aids of digital content.
>
> *Plain language guidelines (Centre for plain language, US)*
>
> - Write for your audience. Use language your audience knows and feels comfortable with. Take your audience's current level of knowledge into account.
> - Address separate audiences separately. By addressing different audiences in the same place, you make it harder for each audience to find the material that applies to them.
> - Address one person, not a group. Remember that even though your document may affect a thousand or a million people, you are speaking to the one person who is reading it. When your writing reflects this, it's more economical and has a greater impact.
> - Organisation is key. Start by stating the document's purpose and its bottom line. Eliminate filler and unnecessary content. Put the most important information at the beginning and include background information (when necessary) toward the end.
> - Use lots of useful headings. The best-organized document will still be difficult for users to follow if they can't see how it's organized. An effective way to reveal your document's organization is to use lots of useful headings.
> - When writing, be precise and concise. Use the active voice – it makes it clear who is supposed to do what. It eliminates ambiguity about responsibilities. Don't complicate things by using words your audience won't understand or abbreviations that confuse them. Write short sentences.
>
> Source: OECD (2021[24]), OECD Report on Public Communication: The Global Context and the Way Forward, https://www.oecd-ilibrary.org/governance/oecd-report-on-public-communication_22f8031c-en; Government of the United States (2010), Federal plain language guidelines, https://www.plainlanguage.gov/guidelines/

Box 2.13. Good practices of communicating about a participatory process

Encouraging participation through communication in Poland

In 2021, the Poznań Citizens' Assembly convened 65 randomly selected citizens in order to deliberate about its response to the climate crisis. The assembly hit a national record in terms of registrations partly by deploying a creative, diverse, and inclusive communications strategy:

- Communication started even before recruitment, via a sub-page in the municipal website and social media platforms, keeping the language as informal as possible.
- Two types of content were pursued: basic facts about the Citizens' Assembly, and constant updates concerning its developments, aiming for the larger audience to follow its journey.
- Communications were diversified: beyond written articles, they also commissioned artists to produce visual aids, published audio recordings of information sessions, and hired a small film-making studio to produce short clips with key facts.
- Attempted to make the process a city-wide event by publishing as much as possible on the city website and on their official Facebook and YouTube accounts, with some limited efforts on more traditional media, like posters.

Expanding public learning beyond participants in Ireland and France

An example of how public communication expands public learning beyond the participants of the process is the Irish Citizens' Assembly of 2016-2018. The initiative was communicated to the public throughout the whole process. Specific outreach activities included streaming discussions online and interviews with participants in the press, radio, and television. Radio interviews allowed participants to discuss their experiences and the public to hear from citizens like them, which helped to build support for the citizen-driven nature of the process. Public communicators and organisers of the process engaged with journalists to echo and amplify participants' discussions. Media coverage was especially helpful in presenting the nuances of this national debate. A similar strategy was adopted by the French Government when organizing the French Citizen Convention on Climate, which benefitted from a very important media coverage, including television, radio, print and social media outlets.

Source: OECD (2021[24]), OECD Report on Public Communication: The Global Context and the Way Forward, https://www.oecd-ilibrary.org/governance/oecd-report-on-public-communication_22f8031c-en; Nowak, Suzanna (2021), Communicating about Citizens' Assemblies: Lessons from the Citizens' Assembly in Poznan, Poland, OECD Participo blog, https://medium.com/participo/communicating-about-citizens-assemblies-2ad0195541d9

Box 2.14. Questions to answer when planning and executing a communications strategy:

- What will be the communications strategy before, during, and after the participation process?
- Which channels will you use to communicate with participants?
- How will you ensure that citizens who are not directly involved in the process are informed about what happens?

Step 7: Implementing a participatory process

The implementation of a participatory process largely depends on the method chosen. Key elements of each model are outlined in the previous section with more detail and guidance on each method available in **Chapter 4**. There are some general considerations that concern any participatory process – such as preparing an adequate timeline, identifying the needed resources, ensuring inclusion and accessibility, and considering a citizens' journey through a participatory process. This section provides tips to support practitioners, public servants, and policy makers throughout the implementation of their participatory process.

Tip 1: Preparing an adequate timeline

- **Planning sufficient time to implement the participation process**. Simpler processes such as public consultations might take a couple of months to implement – from preparing necessary materials, to communicating and inviting citizens to participate, and giving them enough time to provide their contributions. More complex processes, such as participatory budgets, citizen science projects or deliberative processes can take much longer, depending on their scale. For example, for a deliberative process, several months are required to get stakeholders and decision makers on board, around two months to conduct a process of random selection of participants, and several months of learning and deliberation of participants (as they meet every or every other weekend).
- **Aligning the participatory process with the decision-making process.** Participation should be timely in order to inform decision making.
- **Preparing a detailed timeline**. It should include preparatory steps, such as booking the venue and preparing information material, as well as steps to implement the process (how long in-person sessions will be, how much time in between etc.).

Box 2.15. Question to answer when preparing the timeline

- How much time do think will be needed to implement your participatory process properly?
- What are the main steps, and how much time do they take?
- Does the timing of the participation process align with the decision-making process?

Tip 2: Identifying the resources needed

Every participatory process requires dedicated resources to be successfully implemented and result in useful outputs for decision makers. The necessary resources vary depending on the design and implementation of the process. Some elements that will influence the amount and type of resources needed can include: the scope of the process (timeframe, number of participants), the method used, the type of recruitment, the tools, and some logistical considerations such as venues and facilitation. Resources can be human, financial, and/or technical; and can be complemented by partnerships with civil society.

Human resources

Participatory processes (even when completely virtual) require sufficient staff to organise the process, recruit participants, develop information resources, facilitate interactions, answer requests, communicate, analyse and synthesise the inputs, etc. These human resources can be available within your team, such as partners and colleagues, or through external contractors. The quantity and profiles of staff required will depend on the method used, the scope of the process, and the desired input from citizens. Some of the key competences required for any method are project management and communications.

Financial resources

As with every democratic process, participatory processes need dedicated financial resources to cover the cost of human resources, meeting venues and catering, digital platform licenses, public communication, honorarium payments to participants (recommended for some methods of participation), costs of participants' childcare or transport, etc. The costs will depend on internal resources available, the scope of the process, the method, etc. A process that is truly inclusive and breaks down the common barriers to participation will require a larger investment.

Technical resources

More and more processes are using digital tools for communication, receiving participants' inputs, and/or processing/analysing the inputs received (please see Step 5 on p51 of these Guidelines for recommended digital tools). Technical resources can encompass staff with digital skills, software licenses, computers, tablets, cloud services, etc.

Institutional structures

Participation competence centres, advisors, institutional coordinators, or communities of practice as well as context or policy area specific guidance, methodologies, and established platforms might be at your disposal. It is helpful to tap into these resources, especially when implementing a participation process for the first time.

> **Box 2.16. Questions to answer when identifying available resources**
>
> - How many staff (internal/external) will you need to implement the process? How many are available in your organisation?
> - What is your estimated budget?
> - Which technical resources will be needed to implement your process? Can you use existing platforms or tools?
> - What institutional structures and resources are available for use?

Tip 3: *Partnering with non-governmental stakeholders*

In addition to the resources needed to implement a participatory process, public authorities can build alliances and partnerships with non-governmental stakeholders such as civil society organisations (CSOs), the media, or private sector entities. These partnerships can help implement the process, broaden the targeted public, increase the impact of communication efforts, etc. For example, CSOs can help public authorities to reach groups beyond the usual suspects (e.g., migrants), disseminate the opportunities to participate through their networks or regular newsletters, and can be a source of potential resources to implement the process (e.g., facilitators).

> **Box 2.17. Questions to answer when partnering with non-governmental stakeholders**
>
> - Are there any potential partnerships that could be built with civil society? Private sector entities? Media outlets?
> - How can they help you implement your participatory process?

Tip 4: Ensuring inclusion and accessibility

Everyone should have equal opportunities to take part in any participatory process. Section How to motivate citizens to participate? of these guidelines outlines some of the preconditions that enable people to participate and ensure everyone can afford to do so. In addition to that, organisers should ensure that usually underrepresented groups and minorities are represented to effectively address the needs of all citizens. Public authorities should take into consideration any special needs and verify that individuals with disabilities are able to exercise their right to participate in comfort. This includes people using assistive mobility devices (such as wheelchairs, canes, and walkers), individuals with visual and hearing impairments, intellectual disabilities, or other disabilities that reduce their physical and/or sensory fitness.

To ensure an inclusive process:

- Take time when mapping your potential participants to think about the groups of people that usually do not participate, or that are not represented in decision making bodies.
- Reach out beyond the "usual suspects" – for example younger audiences, women, rural populations, minorities, etc.
- Provide information in simple and accessible language for everyone to be able to participate.
- Think about those that do not have access to the internet or to digital devices. If possible, always provide an offline alternative to participate. Non-digital alternatives can be, for example: physical voting, consultations via phone, or any other in-person mechanisms (workshops, kiosks, paper mail, etc.).

To ensure an accessible process:

- Ensuring physical access to participation activities: a person with a disability should be able to reach the meeting place independently. Having an assistant should be a choice, not an obligation. Consider the following aspects: easy access to adequate parking, access from parking to the entrance and through the entrance with assisted mobility devices, ramps/lift available, information in the building adapted for the use of individuals with various disabilities, availability of appropriate equipment during any meetings – such as an induction loop for the hearing impaired, among others.
- Make sure information is accessible to everyone:
    - placing materials sufficiently low, at a height adapted to the capabilities of people in wheelchairs;
    - website design should be in accordance with accessibility standards;
    - providing a sign language interpreter at meetings and hearing aids or additional information on the screen, accompanying the voice message;

- conducting information meetings in easily accessible places or using places without access barriers.

> **Box 2.18. Questions to answer when ensuring accessibility and inclusion**
>
> - Does **everyone** have an equal opportunity to access and participate?
> - What can be done to enhance inclusivity and accessibility to the participatory process?

Tip 5: Thinking as a citizen

One way to ensure that the process will be successful in recruiting participants and maintaining their interest throughout is by putting yourself in the shoes of the target public.

When thinking about the citizens' journey through a participatory process, organisers can anticipate blind spots that could potentially confuse or demotivate participants and reduce dropouts by making necessary adjustments. Figure 2.5 below maps the simplified version of a citizens' experience throughout such a process.

Involve published research and evidence on how and why people participate, which can be a useful start for thinking about the citizen journey.

Figure 2.5. Citizens' journey through a participatory process

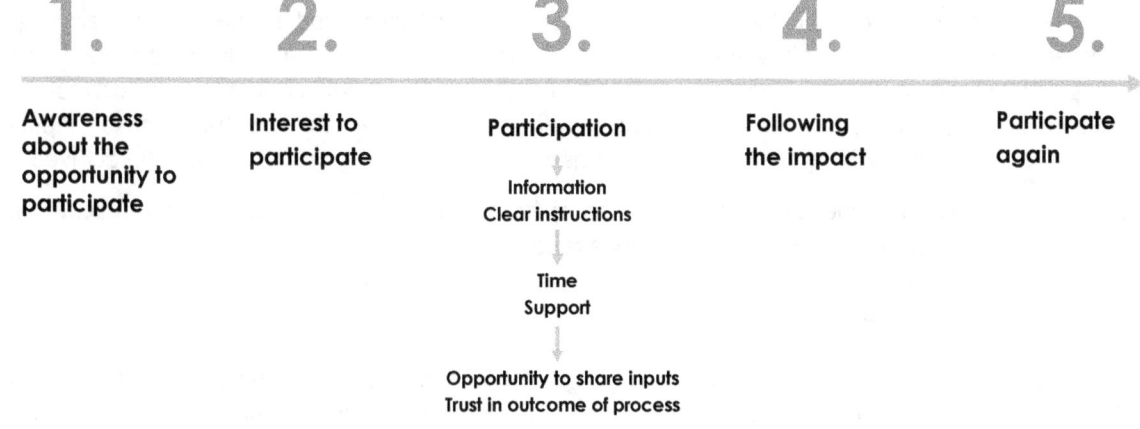

Source: Author's own elaboration

> **Box 2.19. Questions to answer when thinking as a citizen**
>
> - How to raise awareness about the opportunity to participate?
> - How to transform awareness about the participation opportunity into interest?
> - How to move from interest to actual participation and capture commitment?
> - How to keep participants engaged until the end of the process?
> - How to ensure they stay informed about how their input impacted public decisions?
> - How to maintain their interest for future opportunities?

Step 8: Using citizen input and providing feedback

Getting back to participants and the broader public about the results of the participatory process is an important step. It is also one that is often neglected. Without proper acknowledgement of the work and commitment from citizens and stakeholders, participants might get the wrong message that their input was not important or will not be considered, creating distrust and discouraging them from participating in similar activities in the future. Participants should also know which of their recommendations will be taken into account and why some of them might not be used. This increases the transparency and accountability of the process and contributes to building an open government culture.

Taking into account the results of the participatory process

The inputs received as part of the participatory process should be given careful and respectful consideration and used as set out in the beginning – with clear justifications and arguments if certain results are not used or implemented. Public authorities are not obliged to implement all of the recommendations, ideas, or proposals, nor to use all of the data gathered – as long as such choice is justified and corresponds to the initial commitment. It is possible for public authorities to establish that the process is purely consultative, or to commit to integrate certain recommendations, or to integrate all the inputs received.

The important aspect is to be clear and transparent from the beginning, and to communicate with participants and the wider public about the decisions taken.

Closing the feedback loop

Closing the feedback loop refers to the efforts taken by the conveners of a participatory process to get back to participants about the status of their inputs and the ultimate outcome of their participation. By not properly closing the feedback loop, public authorities risk discouraging people from participating another time and potentially diminishing the benefits of participation, such as increased sense of trust, efficacy, and agency.

- After the participatory process, public authorities should get back to participants as well as the broader public with the acknowledgement of the received inputs, recommendations, or help.
- Organisers could explain exactly how the contributions will feed into the bigger picture of the decision making, and when participants can expect any concrete results.
- If some of the proposals cannot be taken into account, then public authorities should be transparent about the reasons. This demonstrates respect for participants and reduces ambiguity and potential misunderstandings.

- Finally, thanking participants for their time and effort, as well as keeping them updated on the progress of the process (and the inputs) can increase a sense of value and appreciation.

> **Box 2.20. Good practice of closing the feedback loop**
>
> **Barcelona's Youth Forum (Spain 2021-2022)**
>
> The Fòrum Jove BCN 2021 (Barcelona Youth Forum) was a representative deliberative process that convened 99 randomly selected people living in Barcelona, Spain aged 16-29 in order to deliberate about the needs of the Barcelonese youth and what the city council could do to help them in their development. They deliberated for five months and issued their recommendations in December 2021.
>
> Less than two months after they delivered their recommendations, on 17 February 2022, representatives from the youth forum and city officials met at the Barcelona town hall for a public event in which they heard from the mayor herself, Ada Colau, explain the next steps regarding their proposals.
>
> The city hall also produced a document that outlined their response for each of the youth forum's 22 recommendations. They accepted 18 of them, they found that they were already doing two of them and they provided their rationale for rejecting the last two. This document was sent to all forum members in March. In addition, they created a commission with representatives from the forum to ensure proper follow-up and evaluate the uptake of the recommendations.
>
> More information can be found at: https://www.decidim.barcelona/processes/forumjoveBCN?locale=es

> **Box 2.21. Questions to answer when closing the feedback loop**
>
> - Who will respond to the participants' inputs and recommendations? What form will this take?
> - How will you recognise and celebrate the work of the participants?
> - How will you communicate the response to the recommendations? And when?

Step 9: Evaluating the participation process

Why evaluate?

Evaluation allows to measure and demonstrate the quality and neutrality of a participatory process to the broader public. This can increase trust and legitimacy in the use of citizen participation for public decision making. Evaluation creates an opportunity for learning by providing evidence and lessons for public authorities and practitioners about what went well, and what did not. It gives a basis for the iteration and improvement of the design and implementation of a participation process (OECD, 2021[25]).

How to evaluate?

Tina Nabatachi (2012[26]) suggests that evaluation is mostly about evaluating the process or the impact of a participatory process:

- **Process evaluations** can help public authorities better understand and improve the implementation and management of a citizen participation process.

- **Impact evaluations** can help public authorities determine whether the citizen participation process reached its intended audience and produced its intended effects.

Evaluation should be planned for from the very start of designing a participatory process. Depending on the method of participation and scale of the participation process, different types of evaluations can be chosen. For a short, small-scale process, such as a public consultation, a participant questionnaire administered by the organisers would be an appropriate evaluation. Whereas for participatory budgeting or representative deliberative processes it is recommended to commission an independent evaluation. In principle, the evaluation should be carried out by people who are not involved in the participatory process, and are thus able to objectively indicate what went according to plan and what did not work. The initiators or commissioners of the participatory process should also reflect on the activities carried out.

Well conducted evaluations can shed light on questions such as:

- What are the main lessons from implementing a participation process?
- Did the participation process go as planned and intended?
- Did it meet its goals?
- Did the decision maker uphold their commitment?
- What worked what did not?
- How did the participants experience the process?

The results of evaluation should have a real impact on the design of other processes in the future.

To design a participant questionnaire, guide self-reflections of the organisers or commission an independent evaluation, it is central to keep in mind the principles for quality participation, which can serve as a benchmark. **Chapter 3** of this document outlines these principles. Further resources on evaluation can be found in **Chapter 4** of the Guidelines.

> Box 2.22. Questions to answer when evaluating a process
>
> - How are you going to evaluate the participation process? When will the evaluation happen?
> - What methods will be used?
> - What criteria will you be using for evaluation?
> - Who will be responsible for the evaluation?

Step 10: Fostering a culture of participation

As part of an open government, citizen participation requires a change of behaviour and mindset to put citizens at the heart of any public action and decision. This involves changes in individual and institutional values, skills, beliefs, norms of conduct, and expectations, which are materialised in new policies, services, and methodologies, among others. At the institutional level, it requires a new set of processes to transform the internal ways of working, and new norms and values that integrate open government and participatory practices as the new normal. At the individual level, it means new ways of thinking about public service and adapting skills to deliver public action in a transparent, accountable, and participatory manner. At all levels, the cultural change requires an adapted mindset that understands the benefit of citizens' inputs (OECD, forthcoming[27]).

Moving from ad hoc process to a participatory culture requires that involving citizens becomes a habit for public authorities. To build this habit, participatory processes should be embedded in the institutional architecture, through legislation or regulation. Besides a change in the public decision making and the mindset of public authorities, a culture of participation requires democratically-fit citizens that are interested and have the agency and needed skills to participate.

Moving from ad hoc practices to institutionalised mechanisms

To support the use of participatory practices and make sure it goes beyond one-off initiatives that are often dependent on political will, efforts should be made to institutionalise them in a structural way. Structural changes to make participation an integral part of the democratic architecture is a way to promote true transformation, as institutionalisation anchors follow-up and response mechanisms in regulations. Creating regular opportunities for more people to have a say on public decision making not only improves policies and services, it also scales the positive impact that participation has on people's perception of themselves and others, strengthening societal trust and cohesion (OECD, 2021[20]).

Institutionalising citizen participation practices can also contribute to the creation of participatory infrastructure available for public authorities. For example, consolidated networks of public servants and practitioners with expertise on citizen participation could be easier mobilised when needed. Participatory methods, especially the more innovative ones, can also become easier and less expensive to implement, as costs and resources are saved by not starting from scratch every time (economies of scale). Building institutional know-how about how to commission or conduct a range of citizen participation methods would enable to implement more such processes, opening up decision making to citizens in a genuine and sustained way (OECD, 2022[28]).

Flexing citizens' democratic muscles and civic readiness

Fostering the culture of participation requires not only the opportunities for citizens to participate, but also citizens who are ready to take on this active role in collaborating, co-creating, and making informed decisions together with public institutions. A citizenry that is democratically fit has the mandate, but also skills and competences needed to play an active part in a democratic system. Multiplying the opportunities for citizens to exercise those democratic muscles through practice can help enhance their democratic fitness and strengthen their skills to express disagreement, find compromise with others, self-mobilise, engage in activism, feel and express empathy, practice active listening, effectively express their opinion, and strengthen verbal self-confidence (We Do Democracy, 2022[29]) (MASS LBP, 2022[30]).

Civic space is a prerequisite for effective participation

It is not enough for governments to decide they want to engage more with citizens. They need to create an environment in which this is possible and in which citizens are able and willing to come forward and engage with public officials. This means that individual rights (particularly freedoms of expression, peaceful assembly, association) need to be respected (de jure and de facto), complaint mechanisms need to function, information and data needs to be made available, rule of law needs to be respected, journalists need to be able to analyse and critique government decisions, protesters need to be able to air their views in safety, and CSOs/activists/human rights defenders need to be able to operate without fear of violence, retribution or interference, etc. (OECD, forthcoming[31]).

A non-protected civic space can contribute to a polarized atmosphere, which hinders the quality of the interactions between non-public stakeholders (including citizens, NGOs, media, etc.) and public authorities. The closing of the civic space can have a direct impact on the level of inclusion of participation. As part of the Recommendation on Open Government, the OECD invites countries to protect their vibrant civic spaces (both offline and online) in order to allow for equal, informed, secure, and inclusive participation.

References

Carson, L. and S. Elstub (2019), *Comparing participatory and deliberative democracy*, newDemocracy Foundation, https://www.newdemocracy.com.au/wp-content/uploads/2019/04/RD-Note-Comparing-Participatory-and-Deliberative-Democracy.pdf. [21]

Dalton, R. (2008), *The Good Citizen: How a Younger Generation is Reshaping American Politics*, CQ Press. [6]

Faulkner, W. and C. Bynner (2020), *How to Design and Plan Public Engagement Processes: A Handbook*, What Works Scotland. [1]

GovLab (2019), *COLLECTIVE INTELLIGENCE AND GOVERNING SERIES THE OPEN POLICYMAKING PLAYBOOK*. [13]

International Telecommunication Union (2021), *Digital inclusion*, https://www.itu.int/en/ITU-D/Digital-Inclusion/Pages/about.aspx. [22]

Involve (2005), *People & Participation: How to put citizens at the heart of decision-making*, Beacon Press. [2]

Joint Research Centre, I. (ed.) (2014), *Citizen science and smart cities : report of summit Ispra, 5-7th February 2014*, Publications Office, https://doi.org/10.2788/80461. [14]

Kuser Olsen, V., G. Galloway and M. Ruth (2018), "The Demographics of Public Participation Access When Communicating Environmental Risk", *Human Ecology Review*, Vol. 24/1, https://doi.org/10.22459/her.24.01.2018.06. [7]

MASS LBP (2022), . [30]

MASS LBP (2017), *"How to Run a Civic Lottery: Designing Fair Selection Mechanisms for Deliberative Public Processes"*, MASS LBP, https://static1.squarespace.com/static/55af0533e4b04fd6bca65bc8/t/5aafb4b66d2a7312c182b69d/15 (accessed on 3 March 2020). [9]

Nabatchi, T. (2012), *A Manager's Guide to Evaluating Citizen Participation*, t. [26]

New Zealand Government (2022), *Community Engagement Policy Tool*, https://dpmc.govt.nz/sites/default/files/2022-01/policy-community-engagement-tool-jan22.pdf. [3]

OECD (2022), "Engaging citizens in cohesion policy: DG REGIO and OECD pilot project final report", *OECD Working Papers on Public Governance*, No. 50, OECD Publishing, Paris, https://doi.org/10.1787/486e5a88-en. [28]

OECD (2021), "Eight ways to institutionalise deliberative democracy", *OECD Public Governance Policy Papers*, No. 12, OECD Publishing, Paris, https://doi.org/10.1787/4fcf1da5-en. [20]

OECD (2021), *Evaluation Guidelines for Representative Deliberative Processes*, OECD Publishing, Paris, https://doi.org/10.1787/10ccbfcb-en. [25]

OECD (2021), *OECD Report on Public Communication: The Global Context and the Way Forward*, OECD Publishing, Paris, https://doi.org/10.1787/22f8031c-en. [24]

OECD (2020), *Innovative Citizen Participation and New Democratic Institutions: Catching the Deliberative Wave*, OECD Publishing, Paris, https://doi.org/10.1787/339306da-en. [10]

OECD (2019), *Select a problem-solving approach*, OPSI, https://oecd-opsi.org/guide/problem-solving-approach/ (accessed on 14 April 2022). [4]

OECD (2017), *OECD Budget Transparency Toolkit: Practical Steps for Supporting Openness, Integrity and Accountability in Public Financial Management*, OECD Publishing, Paris, https://doi.org/10.1787/9789264282070-en. [16]

OECD (2017), *Recommendation of the Council on Open Government*, http://acts.oecd.orgRECOMMENDATIONPUBLICGOVERNANCE (accessed on 18 February 2022). [11]

OECD (2016), *Open Government: The Global Context and the Way Forward*, OECD Publishing, Paris, https://doi.org/10.1787/9789264268104-en. [5]

OECD (2007), "Engaging the Public in National Budgeting: A Non-Governmental Perspective", *OECD Journal on Budgeting*. [19]

OECD (forthcoming), *Open Government Scan of Canada*. [27]

OECD (forthcoming), *The Protection and Promotion of Civic Space: the Global Context and the Way Forward*. [31]

OECD and OGP (2019), *Communicating Open Government: A How-To Guide*. [23]

Participatory Budgeting Atlas (2021), *PB data World*, https://www.pbatlas.net/world.html (accessed on 7 March 2022). [17]

Seltzer, E. and D. Mahmoudi (2012), "Citizen Participation, Open Innovation, and Crowdsourcing: Challenges and Opportunities for Planning", *http://dx.doi.org/10.1177/0885412212469112*, Vol. 28/1, pp. 3-18, https://doi.org/10.1177/0885412212469112. [12]

Smith, A., K. Lehman Schlozman and S. Verba (2009), *The Demographics of Online and Offline Political Participation*, Pew Research Center, https://www.pewresearch.org/internet/2009/09/01/the-demographics-of-online-and-offline-political-participation/. [8]

Veeckman, C. et al. (2019), *Communication in Citizen Science: A practical guide to communication and engagement in citizen science*, Scivil. [15]

Véron, P. (2016), *Why Paris is Building the World's Biggest Participatory Budget*, https://newcities.org/why-paris-is-building-the-worlds-biggest-participatory-budget/ (accessed on 21 February 2022). [18]

We Do Democracy (2022), *Democratic fitness*, https://www.wedodemocracy.dk/democracy-fitness-2. [29]

3 Ensuring quality of participation: Guiding Principles for Citizen Participation Processes

This chapter introduces nine principles to ensure quality of citizen participation processes. Methods of citizen participation outlined in these guidelines rely on principles of good practice to ensure their quality: purpose, accountability, transparency, inclusiveness and accessibility, integrity, privacy, information, resources, and evaluation.

Guiding principles for citizen participation processes

Various methods of citizen participation outlined in these guidelines rely on different principles of good practice to ensure their quality. Even though methods have their own specificities, there are general principles to keep in mind when implementing citizen participation activities that can help ensure quality of a participation process. These principles have been developed based on the analysis of good practice principles for each method (for which such principles were available), and the OECD *Guiding Principles for Open and Inclusive Policy Making*.

- New Zealand Principles of Online Engagement (2022[1])
- OECD Good Practice Principles for Representative Deliberative Processes (2020[2])
- OECD Best Practice Principles on Stakeholder Engagement in Regulatory Policy (2017[3])
- East, North, and South Ayrshire Councils Good Practice Principles for Participatory Budgeting (2016[4])
- EU-Citizen Science Good Practice Principles for Citizen Science Projects (2015[5])
- OECD Guiding Principles for Open and Inclusive Policy Making (2010[6])
- IAP2 Core Values of Public Participation (2017[7])

Figure 3.1. Guiding Principles for Citizen Participation Processes

Source: Author's own elaboration.

1) Clarity and impact

The objective of a citizen participation process should be defined from the outset and linked to a defined public problem or challenge. It should aim for a genuine outcome – and whenever possible, citizens and affected communities should be encouraged to set the agenda and propose issues to be addressed by participatory processes. A participatory process should have a clear link to decision making, and participants should be able to perceive their impact on public decisions.

2) Commitment and accountability

Public authorities should be clear about the expected results of the process to manage participants' expectations. There should be a public commitment to respond to or act on participants' recommendations, following up on the use of their inputs in a timely - and when possible public - manner. Public authorities should inform participants and the broader public on how they use the received inputs.

3) Transparency

The participation process should be announced publicly before it begins. There should be full transparency on any applicable decision-making process which will follow the participation process. The process design and all materials, as well as relevant data, should be available to the public in a timely manner. The response to the inputs received from participants and the evaluation after the process should be publicised and have a public communication strategy. Public authorities can make use of public communication mechanisms to increase awareness beyond participants.

4) Inclusiveness and accessibility

Any interested person or stakeholder should be able to participate, and the processes should reflect the diversity of the community. This means that the methods chosen must be appropriate for the intended audience, efforts are made to reduce barriers to participation and to consider how to involve underrepresented groups. Participation can also be encouraged and supported through remuneration, covered expenses, and/or providing or paying for childcare and eldercare.

5) Integrity

The process must have an honest intention. Depending on the scale of the process, there can be oversight by an advisory or monitoring board, and the participation process can be run by an arms' length co-ordinating team that is different from the commissioning authority. Efforts should be made to protect the process from private interests or policy capture by specific interest groups.

6) Privacy

There should be respect for participants' privacy. Any data collected and published should have participants' consent. All participants' personal information and data should be treated in compliance with international good practices, such as the European Union's General Data Protection Regulation (GDPR), and taking into account legal and ethical issues surrounding data collection and sharing, copyright, and intellectual property.

7) Information

Participants should have access to a wide and diverse range of accurate, relevant, and accessible evidence and expertise. Participation processes should be designed to give citizens full (to the extent necessary) and clear knowledge about a specific issue.

8) Resources

Public authorities should secure the necessary resources to properly implement participatory processes. Such resources can be human, financial, and technical. Public authorities might need to call on external expertise, but when possible should build capacities internally to foster a culture of participation. In addition, public officials should have access to appropriate skills, guidance, and training as well as an organisational culture that supports both in-person and online participation.

9) Evaluation

Participation processes should be evaluated to create an opportunity to learn and improve. Evaluation strengthens the trust of policy makers, the public, and stakeholders in any recommendations or other outcomes of participation processes. There should be an anonymous evaluation by the participants to assess the process based on objective criteria and an internal evaluation by the co-ordination team. An independent evaluation is recommended for some participatory processes, particularly those that last a significant time.

References

East, North and South Ayrshire Councils (2016), *Participatory Budgeting Toolkit*. [4]

European Citizen Science Association (2015), *Ten principles of citizen science*. [5]

Government of New Zealand (2022), *Principles of online engagement*. [1]

IAP2 (2017), *IAP2 Core Values of Public Participation*. [7]

OECD (2020), *Good Practice Principles for Deliberative Processes for Public Decision Making*. [2]

OECD (2017), *Best Practice Principles on Stakeholder Engagement in Regulatory Policy*. [3]

OECD (2010), *OECD Guiding Principles for Open and Inclusive Policy Making*. [6]

4 Useful resources

This chapter lists useful resources that can complement the guidance provided by these guidelines.

Databases of various examples of citizen participation

- The OECD database of representative deliberative processes includes close to 600 examples from across the world.
- OECD's Observatory for Public Sector Innovation (OPSI) Case Study Library collects good practices of innovations in government including participatory practices.
- Participedia is a collaborative repository of citizen participation case studies.
- LATINNO database gathers more than 3744 cases of democratic innovations in Latin America.
- People Powered Hub is useful to navigate participatory budgets examples and other citizen participation processes.
- Gov Lab CrowdLaw Catalog is a repository of more than 100 cases from around the world using different methods such as co-creation, or open innovation.
- CitizenLab publishes case studies of digital participatory processes at the local level.

Handbooks & further readings on citizen and stakeholder participation

- How To Design And Plan Public Engagement Processes: A Handbook (What Works Scotland)
- Guide to Public Participation (Environmental Protection Agency)
- Open Policy Making Toolkit (UK Government)
- Good Practice Guide for Community Engagement (New Zealand Government)
- Enabling Active Citizenship: Public Participation in Government into the Future (New Zealand Government)
- The Open Policy Making Playbook (Govlab)
- Community Engagement: a Practitioner's Guide (Citizenlab)
- Knowledge Base (Involve Uk)
- Stakeholder Participation Guide (Initiative for Climate Action Transparency)

OECD publications

- Citizens as Partners: OECD Handbook on Information, Consultation and Public Participation in Policy-Making (2001)
- Innovative Citizen Participation and New Democratic Institutions: Catching the Deliberative Wave (2020).
- OECD Handbook on Open Government for Peruvian Civil Servants (2020)
- Eight ways to institutionalise deliberative democracy (2021)
- Evaluation Guidelines for representative deliberative processes (2021)

Good practice principles

- OECD Good Practice Principles for Representative Deliberative Processes
- OECD Guiding Principles for Open and Inclusive Policy Making
- EU-Citizen.Science Good Practice Principles for Citizen Science Projects
- CIVICUS Good Practice Principles for Public Consultations

- East, North, and South Ayrshire Councils Good Practice Principles for Participatory Budgeting
- New Zealand Principles of online engagement

Blogs and podcasts

- OECD Participo
- A Framework of Open Practices
- The Living Library – Gov Lab

Resources on how to identify a public problem

- OECD's Observatory for Public Sector Innovation on "Select a problem-solving approach"
- New York University, GovLab's Public Problem Solving Canvas
- OECD's Innovative Citizen Participation and New Democratic Institutions: Catching the Deliberative Wave section on Scope of the remit

Resources on identifying participants and recruitment processes

- Nesta's Collective Intelligence Design Playbook includes a series of helpful tools to facilitate such a mapping exercise.
- MASS LBP's How to run a civic lottery provides guidance and practical support on random selection.
- New Zealand Government's Guide to Inclusive Community Engagement guides government agencies and policy advisors on how to increase inclusion in participatory practices.
- Involve's Who to Involve? highlights important questions for the participant selection stage.

Resources on using digital tools for participation

- People Powered Guide to Digital Participation Platforms is a practical guide on how to design a digital participatory process and select the right tool.
- Involve's Where do I start with digital engagement? Is a guide to help practitioners build a digital process, and digital tools database.
- CitizenLab's e-Participation canvas is short e-book providing a framework for internal use for the development of a digital citizens' participation platform.
- IBM Center for The Business of Government Using Online Tools to Engage - and be Engaged by - the Public is a practical report mapping and detailing how to best use online tools to engage with the public.
- NESTA's Digital Democracy: The Tools Transforming Political Engagement shares lessons from different experiences of digital democracy put forth by different European governments.
- NESTA's What is next for democratic innovations looks at barriers to embed digital participatory processes into institutions.
- ERDF's Digital Democracy: A Guide on Local Practices of Digital Participation gives advice for implementation of digital tools for governance, specifically at the local and regional level.

- NewDemocracy and Democratic Society's Designing an Online Public Deliberation explains how to build tools for online deliberation that do not simply mirror offline deliberation, but that are better adapted for the digital space.
- MySociety's Digital Tools for Citizens' Assemblies explores how digital tools can be used to enhance in-person CAs.
- New Zealand's How to engage with people online is a step-by-step guide to engaging with people online — from creating an engagement strategy to closing the engagement.
- The Council of Europe BePART platform provides learnings for participatory formats and tools

Resources on communication

- *The OECD* Report on Public Communication: The Global Context and the Way Forward examines the public communication structures, mandates and practices of centres of governments and ministries of health from 46 countries.
- The OECD and OGP's Communicating Open Government – A How-To Guide is a resource for individuals tasked with explaining, encouraging, and building support for open government.
- RSA's Reporting on and telling the story of a Citizens' Assembly helps commissioning bodies, including local authorities, to communicate, report the events, and tell the story of a citizens' assembly.
- PB Outreach Toolkit is a guide to plan and execute effective outreach campaigns for participatory budgeting processes.

Resources on inclusion and accessibility

- Simon Fraser University's Beyond Inclusion: Equity in Public Engagement proposes eight principles to support the meaningful and equitable inclusion of diverse voices in public engagement processes across sectors.

Resources on evaluation

- OECD's Evaluating Public Participation in Policy Making examines the key issues for consideration when evaluating information, consultation and public participation.
- OECD's Evaluation Guidelines for Representative Deliberative Processes
- InterAct's Evaluating participatory, deliberative and co-operative ways of working provides examples from experience in the field, and further development of criteria and indicators for good practice.
- Institute on Governance's Evaluating Citizen Engagement in Policy Making suggests a framework to evaluate participatory processes.

Resources and guidance on open meetings / Townhall meetings

Open meetings and town hall meetings are participatory tools that can be traced all the way back to 17th-century New England meetings or colonial traditions in Latin America (cabildos). Now these processes are used worldwide, most often at local or legislative level, to foster information about public action, encourage citizen participation and to build a relationship based on accountability and trust.

Contrary to a public consultation, an open meeting or town hall meeting does not seek to gather inputs on a particular issue. These processes are rather a means for public authorities to start a discussion with the public, whether to understand their needs, present upcoming decisions or share advances of implemented actions. They also help maintain a direct channel for communication and be accountable to the public on certain actions or mandates. As open meetings and town hall meetings are not designed to be representative, they can be organized fairly easily in four steps.

A more detailed description can be consulted in **Chapter 2.**

Table 4.1. Steps of an open meeting/town hall meeting

Step	Description
Step 1: Define the topic(s) to discuss	Because public authorities are not in principle bound by any of what may come out of those discussions, the topic and framing of the meeting can be rather loose. The objective is to find a purpose precise enough to enable discussion, present evidence and provide information, in order for the public to be able to participate in the debate. Sometimes, public authorities allow the public to propose topics to the agenda or present initiatives and projects.
Step 2: Communicate	Public authorities should announce the date, time, and location of the meeting with sufficient time to allow citizens and stakeholders to participate. The publicity for these meetings is generally done both in-person and via digital means, in order to reach a broader audience. Although the very nature of open meetings and town hall meetings involve non-representative attendants, efforts should be made to make them as inclusive as possible.
Step 3: Hold the meeting	These meetings can be organized in any physical space available, often in places linked to public authorities (town halls, public amphitheaters, schools, libraries, squares, etc.). More recently, and especially during the Covid-19 pandemic, these meetings have been organized in virtual spaces, a trend that may continue. Regarding the agenda of the meeting, public authorities usually start with and opening remark presenting the agenda and topics to be discussed, followed by a discussion with participants. Ensure sufficient time for participants to ask questions and for public authorities to answer. When opening the floor to participants, it is important to moderate the discussion and encourage an equal and (as much as possible) representative distribution of the floor.
Step 4: Keep records	A written record should be published to allow for more transparency, accountability and to engage with a broader public.
Step 5: Follow up	It is highly recommended that public authorities follow up with participants (and the wider public) about the outcomes of the meeting, especially if decisions were taken. Public authorities can communicate about the topics discussed, the main questions raised, and the answers provided (as a FAQ).

Source: Author's own elaboration.

- Involve's Guide to 21st Century Town Meeting provides practical information to support public authorities in organizing public meetings using digital and in-person mechanisms.
- The United States Environmental Protection Agency's Guide to Public Participation provides guidance to organise successful public participation, with specific elements on open meetings.
- CIVICUS published factsheets on Public Forums and Town Hall Meetings, providing guidance and important information for public authorities interested in organizing public and open meetings.

Resources and guidance on public consultations

A consultation is a two-way relationship in which citizens provide feedback to a public institution (such as comments, perceptions, information, advice, experiences, and ideas). Usually, governments define the issues for consultation, set the questions, and manage the process, while citizens and/or stakeholders are invited to contribute their views and opinions.

A more detailed description can be consulted in **Chapter 2.**

Table 4.2. Steps of a public consultation

Step	Description
Step 1: Define purpose and scope	Before the consultation is launched, public authorities should define: • The purpose of the consultation: for example, to gather ideas, understand public opinion about a topic, test draft solutions, collect feedback, etc. • The type of desired inputs: ideas, comments, expert advice, etc. • Expected participants: citizens (small vs. large groups), experts (i.e. scientists), targeted populations (i.e. seniors, LGBTI, etc.)
Step 2: Select a consultation method	Public consultations are not a one-fits-all type of method. Depending on the answers of Step 1, public authorities should select an appropriate method: • Comment periods • Focus groups • Surveys • Public Opinion Polls • Workshops/seminars/conferences/round-table discussions • Stakeholder interviews See Table 2.4 for more details about each method.
Step 3: Deciding if digital or in-person	Depending on the scope, expected outcomes, and the method chosen, public authorities can decide if the public consultation will be held online, in-person or in a hybrid setting.
Step 4: Communicate about consultation	Once the design is set, public authorities should communicate widely about the process, ensuring their expected participants are reached. Digital channels such as social media can be effective to attract all types of citizens, especially digitally native and young publics; specialised media can be helpful to target specific stakeholders, billboards or traditional media can be useful when reaching to all types of citizens or residents of a certain area. Organizers should be clear about the expected outcome of the consultation and their level of commitment to include inputs in the final decision.
Step 5: Consult	For effective and meaningful participation, organizers should ensure that all participants have: • Sufficient time • Required information • Clear instructions • Support in case of need (human or technical)
Step 6: Close the feedback loop	Once the consultation is closed, organizers should communicate to participants and the wider public about the results of the process. This means sharing if and how the public authority will use the inputs received. This is important to maintain interest for future consultations.

Source: Author's own elaboration.

- More on focus groups
- The European Commission's Guidelines on Stakeholder Consultation provides definitions of key terms, motivations for consultation and a method for doing so.
- The OECD's Background Document on Public Consultation provides definitions, methods and examples from OECD countries, along with good practices.
- CitizenLab published two short e-books on public consultations, with special emphasis on digital engagement: The FAQs of Digital Consultation and 6 Methods for Online Consultation.
- Consultation Principles utilized by the UK Government (2013).
- BRE UK's Code of Practice on Consultation includes seven criteria to guide policy makers on when and how to conduct stakeholder consultation.
- The Irish Governments' Consultation Principles & Guidance provides principles and also advice on practical issues that may arise throughout a consultation procedure.

Resources and guidance on open innovation

There are several types of open innovation methods available for public authorities.

Crowdsourcing usually involves a digital platform where participants can publish ideas or contributions to answer the organizing authority's request or question. In-person alternatives can be put in place, such as workshops or boxes to gather ideas.

Hackathons are usually in-person events organized throughout a weekend, in a shared space where all participants can work and share ideas. Hackathons are sprint-oriented events, so the goal is to allow for a collaborative work environment with technical facilities and usually involve a setting the scene moment and a pitch session where participants present their ideas and solutions. Participants work in teams to solve one or several problems and mentors with strong expertise on the policy problem or the type of solution expected can be assign to each team. In some occasions, public authorities might consider rewarding the winner(s) with a prize or the recognition that comes with the implementation of their idea as a policy solution. For a hackathon to be productive, public authorities should put data and information about the problem to solve at disposal of participants.

Public challenges are usually based on a digital platform where public authorities publish a public problem to solve and call for citizens or stakeholders to propose a solution. In some cases, public authorities can organise in-person sessions to answer questions or provide coaching and support to improve the participants solutions.

Table 4.3. Steps for Open Innovation

Key step	Description
Step 1: Pick a challenge	Decide on and frame the problem(s) to solve by participants.
Step 2: Choose the method	Decide on the conditions to participate (online, in-person) and the profiles of participants you will need to attract.
Step 3: Invite participants	Communicate clearly about the problem, the conditions to participate and the expected goal of the process (depending on the method – inviting people to share ideas online or to form a team and come to an in-person event).
Step 4: Prepare	Decide on criteria to select the winners of the public challenge and communicate the criteria widely before the selection process starts. If a hackathon is organised, nominate a jury that will judge the final solutions designed

	by participants. The jury can be a mix of public authorities as well as independent jury members from civil society or academia. Gather (and share with participants) sufficient data and information regarding the problem you are aiming to solve.
Step 5: Implement	Allow for enough time for participants to work on a proposal. Provide necessary support, such as mentorship, expert advice. For in-in person hackathons, organise a final presentation session for participants to pitch their solutions to the jury and the broader public. Select, acknowledge, and award the best ideas.
Step 6: Close the feedback loop	Communicate about the implementation status of the solutions.
Step 7: Sustainability	Consider mechanisms to make the solutions identified sustainable in the medium to long term (replicability, incubation, etc.)

Source: Author's own elaboration

- Mozilla Foundation's A Framework of Open Practices describes and provides guidance on how to use open and collaborative innovation methods based on the experience of Mozilla and other innovative organisations.
- The United Kingdom's Open Policy Making Toolkit includes information about Open Policy Making as well as the tools and techniques policy makers can use to create more open and user led policy.
- The Power of Hackathons: a roadmap for sustainable open innovation by Zachary Bastien provides an overview of hackathons and offers practical guidance as well as good practices from successful experiences.
- The United States' 21st-Century Public Servants: Using Prizes and Challenges to Spur Innovation presents results and experiences from the Obama Administration approach of using public challenges to solve complex public problems and other innovative methodologies. Better
- GovLab's Open Policy Making Playbook offers case studies and guidance for policy-makers to include collaborative and innovative approaches to policy making.

Resources and guidance on citizen science

Citizen science is an involvement of citizens in scientific research. By doing so researchers, citizens, and sometimes policy makers come together to tackle scientific and policy problems. Through citizen science, citizens can participate in many stages of the scientific process, from the design of the research question, to data collection and volunteer mapping, data interpretation and analysis, and to publication and dissemination of results (eu-citizen.science, 2022[1]). Citizen science allows researchers to tap into scientific curiosity and resources of citizens to achieve scientific results, all the while creating opportunities for citizens to learn about a specific issue or research question and discover scientific processes.

Table 4.4. Steps for Citizen Science

Step	Description
Step 1: Define the purpose	The process starts by determining the purpose of involving citizens in a public research or a scientific project. What is the role that citizens and/or stakeholders will play? For example: - Gather data or evidence to fill an existing gap - Determine or define research questions - Co-create the research design
Step 2: Establish a roadmap	The next step is to establish a clear plan, which outlines the steps and how citizens will be engaged. A good practice is to keep the citizens' participation journey in mind. For example, if citizens are collecting and analysing

	data, they should be kept informed how the data is used, and the final research results. If citizens have a more active role of determining the research questions or co-creating the research design, they should be kept up to date about the following steps that the project takes.
Step 3: Recruit participants	Participants in citizen science are usually volunteers recruited via an open call. Depending on the type of projects, a recruitment strategy might target specific groups, such as schools or students, people with particular interests or living in specific locations, or the general public at large. To recruit a sufficient number of motivated participants, a communication plan is essential.
Step 4: Implement	Depending on the nature of the citizen science initiative, implement workshops with citizens to engage them in setting research questions, provide citizens with necessary training or tools to collect data etc.
Step 5: Publish results and communicate	Providing clear and accessible information about the process and the research will help ensure citizens' engagement and learning. Besides being transparent with participants, public authorities should communicate the results of the research with the wider public to increase uptake of the findings, and recognise the participation of the community.

Source: Author's own elaboration.

- SCivil Guides and manuals includes a guide to getting started with citizen science, explaining all the most basic details and also a manual on communication around a citizen science project.
- GEWISS Citizen science for all presents a guide for citizen science, both its practical and theoretical aspects in fields ranging from education to arts and humanities.
- Digital Tools is a compilation of useful resources, including software, academic literature, links to conferences, among many other practical tools.

Resources and guidance on civic monitoring

Public institutions can largely benefit from creating feedback channels for citizens to provide inputs, comments and complaints to improve the decisions, actions, and services. When involving citizens and stakeholders in the oversight and evaluation of decisions and actions, public authorities can create virtuous circles and healthier relationships that can contribute to the overall trust in government.

Civic monitoring can be implemented using a diverse set of methods, such as:

- Public opinion surveys
- Citizen Report Cards
- Social Audits
- Citizen complaints mechanisms
- Community-based monitoring and evaluation
- Public expenditure tracking
- Online tools
- Representative deliberative processes

The steps to implement can change significantly depending on the chosen tool. The table below suggest some general steps to implement a civic monitoring process:

Table 4.5. Steps for implementing a civic monitoring process

Step	Description

Step 1: Take civic monitoring into consideration while designing a policy or service	Even though civic monitoring generally takes place at the evaluation stage of the policy-cycle, its use should be taken into account at the policy formulation stage in order to allocate all of the necessary resources for its implementation.
Step 2: Define the scope of your expectations	Define the type of feedback you would like to receive from citizens. This will vary according to your own context and whether you are implementing a policy or providing a service. For instance: • Specific, targeted complaints when a service malfunctions; • Constant monitoring for enhanced accountability; • Detailed recommendations about how to improve a public policy or service. This will also help determine the most appropriate method to implement.
Step 3: Choose a methodology	Decide which method you would like to implement, according to your context and what would be most appropriate given the policy or service. Refer to **Table 2.5. Typology of civic monitoring mechanisms** for more details on each of them.
Step 4: Communicate about it	Ensure that citizens and stakeholders have clear knowledge where they can express their feedback. For instance, you could use social media to promote a digital tool, or organise town hall meetings to announce the launching of a Citizen Report Card initiative.
Step 5: Implement the chosen method	Depending on the specific method, this could range from setting up a dedicated website to receive complaints, publishing budgetary information for public scrutiny, or organising a representative deliberative process. Whatever the method, make sure to leave enough time for feedback and to be ready to incorporate it into public action.
Step 6: Integrate feedback into policy or service delivery	Lastly, make sure to take received feedback into account at an appropriate time, whether when updating policy or tweaking service delivery. Communicate about any changes in order to close the feedback loop.

Source: Author's own elaboration

- NYU's Crowd Law Guide includes a section on how to involve citizens and stakeholders in the evaluation of policies and legislations, including through social auditing and online tools.
- CIVICUS published a series of fact-sheets providing guidance and important information for public authorities interested in implementing participatory processes in the evaluation of policies and services:
    - Fact-sheet on Social Audits
    - Fact-sheet on Community Based Monitoring System
    - Fact-sheet on Public Expenditure Tracking
    - Fact-sheet on Community Monitoring and Evaluation
    - Fact-sheet on Citizen Report Cards
- International Budget Project's Citizen's Guide to Monitoring Government Expenditures is a useful resource to support civic monitoring of the budget cycle.

Resources and guidance on participatory budgeting

There is not a one-fits-all solution for participatory budgets, as each public institution can accommodate the process to fit its desired purpose, timeline or legal requirements. However, there are certain stages that all participatory budgets should include:

Table 4.6. Steps for implementing a participatory budget

Step	Description
Step 1: Define details and scope of process	Before the process is open for participation, public authorities should establish the scope of the process, the expected outcomes, the stages of the process as well as the conditions for the projects to be eligible.

	To be able to communicate about the process, public authorities should have decided the following elements: • Budget allocated for the process • Public that will be able to participate • Criteria for eligibility of proposals • Stages of the process • Timings for the different stages
Step 2: First stage of decision making: proposals	In this initial stage, public authorities invite citizens and stakeholders to make proposals (projects, ideas, topics, etc.) that will then be voted and implemented. Before launching the call for proposals, organizers should make the rules of the game clear: • **Who can present proposals?** It can be open to all citizens and stakeholders, to only a certain category of citizens (target groups) or stakeholders (NGOs, associations, etc.), or it can be the government that makes the proposals. • **Which proposals are accepted?** This is important for participants to know in advance the specificities to take into account when submitting a proposal. Public authorities can define prior to the process certain conditions such as budget constraints, feasibility, locality of proposal, duration of implementation, etc. It is also important to decide on the methodology and format to submit the proposals: • **In-person:** Some processes require citizens and stakeholders to co-create the proposals through in-person mechanisms such as workshops, hackathons, town hall meetings, makerspaces, etc. • **Online:** The vast majority of participatory budgets put in place a digital platform where the public can submit their proposals. • **Hybrid:** To maximise inclusion and fairness, some processes put in place a hybrid system where citizens and stakeholders can submit their proposals both though a digital platform or an in-person mechanism.
Step 3: Evaluation of proposals and feasibility	In some participatory budgets, public authorities decide to include an intermediate stage between the submission and the vote, to review the proposals and decide on their feasibility. This analysis has to be transparent, meaning that the public authority should communicate about the conditions for proposals to be accepted. Once the submissions are reviewed, the authority can publish the proposals that are accepted and put to vote. This evaluation can be done by different types of stakeholders; namely: • A group of experts • A randomly selected group of citizens • Public authorities
Step 4: Second stage of decision making: vote	In this stage, the proposals that have been accepted by the public authorities are submitted to a vote in order to select the ones that will be implemented. Once again, the rules of who can participate should be clear as well as the mechanisms available for the public to vote. • **Who can vote?** Public authorities should decide and communicate the individuals that are eligible to participate in the vote. It can go from all residents of a geographical area, to targeted groups. • **How can the public vote?** Public authorities can implement different methodologies: digital platforms, physical booths, SMS voting, mail ballots, or hybrid systems. The ultimate goal should be to ensure that all the eligible participants have the capacity to vote. Once the vote stage is finalized, public authorities should communicate widely about the results.
Step 5: Implementation and evaluation	In some cases, citizens and stakeholders are also involved in the execution of the selected projects or proposals, and in the monitoring and evaluation phases.

	It is highly recommended that participatory budgets become a continuous practice, meaning a process that repeats itself in a continuous basis (yearly, bi-annually, etc.) for citizens to be able to follow up the implementation of the projects and create a culture of participation.

Source: Author's own elaboration

- UN HABITAT's 72 Frequently Asked Questions about Participatory Budgeting provides guidance on how to define a participatory budget, how to implement it, how to decide on the allocation of budget and the participatory aspects.
- East, North and South Ayrshire Councils Participatory Budgeting Toolkit was developed in Scotland for community groups and organizations who are planning to organise a participatory budget.
- Another city is possible with participatory budgeting by Yves Cabannes discusses the background and challenges of PB processes. It highlights 13 cases of PB around the world, in various contexts and institutions. It also includes recommendations to address challenges with participation.
- Great Cities Institute's Participatory Budgeting in Schools: A Toolkit for Youth Democratic Action is a toolkit, developed based on participatory budgeting experiences in Chicago schools, aims to make PB easier to implement with teachers and youth in schools across a wide variety of models and contexts.
- EMPACI Participatory Budgeting (PB) Blueprint Guidebook presents best practices based on case studies.
- People Powered How Cities can use Participatory Budgeting to address Climate Change provides short information sheet giving useful recommendations.
- The Participatory Budgeting World Atlas
- Citizen Lab's An introduction to participatory budgeting
- lesbudgetsparticipatifs is a website with information about participatory budgeting in France that offers expertise and guidance for PB implementers/practitioners.
- Participatory Budgeting Project is a website with useful resources to design, implement and evaluate PBs.
- Text Messaging for Participatory Budgeting explains how participatory budgeting practitioners can use mass text messaging to effectively engage underrepresented communities.
- PB training is a series of video tutorials by Democratic Society to help practitioners navigate different aspects of a participatory budgeting.

Resources and guidance on representative deliberative processes

Representative deliberative processes, such as Citizens' Assemblies, Juries, and Panels, are some of the most innovative citizen participation methods that public authorities from all levels of government increasingly initiate to tackle complex policy problems ranging from climate change to infrastructure investment decisions. The design of these processes varies depending on several factors: the policy issue to be tackled, the level of governance, the number of randomly selected citizens etc. Below is a simplified pathway to designing such a process. Please see the resources below for detailed guidance on every step.

Table 4.7. Steps of a representative deliberative process

Step	Description
Step 1: Commitment and buy-in	Securing buy-in from politicians/policy makers/decision makers. This is a crucial step of the process, which helps to ensure that a citizens' jury or panel is meaningful and will have impact on decision making. It is important to factor in enough time to

		establish this.
Step 2: Identify the issue to solve and frame the question		Before starting the design of the process, it is important to identify the issue or problem that citizens will be asked to solve. Once the issue has been identified, it is important to frame it as a question – using simple and clear language.
Step 3: Design the process		The complexity of the question citizens will be asked to address will affect how many randomly selected citizens will be required, how much time they will need, which experts and stakeholders should provide information, and what online tools could be helpful. It is essential that experts with experience of designing representative deliberative processes are involved in making these design choices.
Step 4: Recruit participants		Once it is clear how many citizens will be selected, how long they will meet for etc., public authorities should recruit participants through civic lottery (please see Civic lottery section of these Guidelines).
Step 5: Prepare for the process		Once citizens are recruited, public authorities should prepare a balanced package of information that citizens will use to base their deliberations on, invite the stakeholders that will present to citizens their diverse points of view on the issue, and brief the facilitators. Identifying broad and diverse information from experts and stakeholders is needed for citizens' to be able to deliberate and reach public judgement. Successful deliberation requires skilled facilitation.
Step 6: Launch the process		A representative deliberative process can vary in terms of time, but they should all follow the following steps: 1. **A team/community building phase**, when the members of the process meet one another and establish the values that will guide their deliberation. During some cases they also receive training on understanding biases and critical thinking. This phase creates the conditions for their deliberation to be possible in the latter stages. 2. **A learning phase**, where citizens become familiar with the policy question and consider a range of perspectives presented by experts, stakeholders, and affected groups, a diverse mix of whom present to the participants in person or in writing and answer their questions. It is also common for citizens to be able to request additional information, experts, or stakeholders if they feel they are missing information or need additional clarifications. For bigger processes, it is common to conduct other participation methods, such as public consultations or crowdsourcing ideas, before a representative deliberative process starts, to gather inputs from the broader public. 3. **Citizen deliberation**, when evidence is discussed, options and trade-offs are assessed, and recommendations are collectively developed. The process is carefully designed to maximise opportunities for every participant to exercise public judgement and requires impartial trained facilitators. 4. **Reaching a "rough consensus"** – finding (as much as possible) a proposal or range of options that a large proportion of participants can strongly agree on. When voting is used, it is either an intermediate step on the way to rough consensus, or a "fall back" mechanism when consensus cannot be reached. 5. **Final recommendations** are made publicly available
Step 7: Public response and follow up		Once the deliberative process is finished and the recommendations have been published and widely communicated, the convening authority should provide a public response to the recommendations. For those recommendations that might not be implemented, public authority should provide clear justifications. For any recommendations that are accepted by the public authority, information about their implementation should be provided regularly to allow citizens to monitor the level of advancement.
Step 8: Evaluate the process		By making a process subject to evaluation, the authorities commissioning it demonstrate a commitment to transparency and quality, earning them greater legitimacy. Evaluation also creates opportunities for learning by providing evidence and lessons for public authorities and practitioners about what went well and what did not. Evaluation should be set up from the beginning of the process, and a final evaluation report should be published after it is over. Please see OECD Evaluation Guidelines for Representative Deliberative Processes for further guidance.

Source: Author's own elaboration

- The OECD Trello board with a range of further resources for representative deliberative processes.
- OECD's Innovative Citizen Participation and New Democratic Institutions: Catching the Deliberative Wave
- OECD's Toolbox and useful resources on Deliberative Democracy.
- OECD's Eight Ways to Institutionalise Deliberative Democracy
- OECD's Evaluation Guidelines for Representative Deliberative Processes
- Handbook on Democracy beyond Elections by UN Democracy Fund & newDemocracy Foundation
- MASS LBP's Guide on How to run a civic lottery
- Citizens' Assemblies: Guide to Democracy That Works by Marcin Gerwin.
- People Powered How to Start a Climate Assembly provides short information sheets with key facts.
- RSA's How to run a Citizen's Assembly is a handbook covering the planning, organizing and delivery stages of a CA.
- Journal of Deliberative Democracy
- Action Catalogue
- Dublin City University's Enhancing Citizen Engagement on the Climate Crisis: The Role of Deliberation is a short and useful guide for policymakers wishing to utilise deliberation to further engage citizens.
- Involve's How do I set up a Citizens' Assembly? is a step by step guide for practitioners.

5 Checklist for designing and planning a citizen participation process

This checklist can be used by any public authority as step-by-step guide through the design and implementation of a participatory process. Further and detailed information about every step is included in the various sections of the guidelines.

Step 1: Identifying the problem to solve and the moment for participation

Where in the project or policy cycle are you? Please select one:

- ☐ issue identification stage
- ☐ policy or project formulation stage
- ☐ decision-making stage
- ☐ implementation stage
- ☐ evaluation stage

What is the problem that citizens (or stakeholders) could help tackle?

How can citizens and/or stakeholders help you solve this problem?

Step 2: Defining the expected results

What type(s) of inputs would you like to receive from participants? Please select one or more:

- ☐ Ideas and proposals
- ☐ Broad opinions
- ☐ Expertise or technical advice
- ☐ Informed recommendations
- ☐ Concrete actions
- ☐ Feedback or alerts
- ☐ Direct decision
- ☐ Evidence
- ☐ Other:

How will you use these inputs to solve the problem you have identified? Please select:

- ☐ Only for consultation
- ☐ We will use it for inspiration
- ☐ We will use it to inform our decision
- ☐ We will implement some of the inputs
- ☐ We will implement all the inputs
- ☐ Not sure yet

Step 3: Identifying the relevant public to involve and recruiting participants

Given the policy issue or public challenge at stake, what groups should be reflected among the participants? Please select one or more:

☐ Representative sample of citizens
☐ A non-representative but diverse group of citizens
☐ A group of citizens with specific skills
☐ Experts and technical profiles
☐ Stakeholders representing diverse opinions (NGOs, business unions, etc.)
☐ Residents of a specific area
☐ A specific group of citizens
☐ Broader public
☐ Other:

Based on needs indicated above, which recruitment method will you use? Please select one:

☐ Open call
☐ Closed call
☐ Civic lottery

How many people should be involved?

How will you ensure – and maintain – the interest of participants throughout the process?

Step 4: Choosing the participation method

Determine which method most closely matches your needs, yields your desired type of inputs, and is feasible given your timeline and resources:

☐ OPEN MEETINGS / TOWN HALL MEETINGS
☐ PUBLIC CONSULTATION
☐ OPEN INNOVATION: CROWDSOURCING, HACKATHONS, AND PUBLIC CHALLENGES
☐ CITIZEN SCIENCE
☐ CIVIC MONITORING
☐ PARTICIPATORY BUDGETING
☐ REPRESENTATIVE DELIBERATIVE PROCESSES

More practical guidance for every method is provided in **Chapter 4**.

Step 5: Choosing the right digital tools

Will you use an online platform and/or a digital tool?

☐ Yes
☐ No

If yes, how would you envision participants using the digital tool in the context of your participatory process?

☐ Proposing new projects, ideas, or suggestions.
☐ Deliberating to agree on shared decisions.
☐ Voting on suggested ideas or projects.
☐ Prioritizing potential options.
☐ Drafting strategies, policies, or legislations.
☐ Sharing information or data to fill an existing gap.
☐ For communication purposes.
☐ Other:

Indicate what digital tool(s) will be used:

How will you ensure that everyone has access and is able to use those tools?

Step 6: Communicating about the process

Think about establishing a strategy to communicate before, during, and after the participation process.

Determine which channels you will use to communicate with participants:

☐ Email
☐ Online private channel (Facebook, Discord, etc.)
☐ Online public channel (Facebook, Twitter, etc.)
☐ Instant messaging applications (WhatsApp, Telegram, Signal, etc.)
☐ Other:

Determine which channels you will use to communicate with the broader public (citizens who are not directly involved in the participation process):

☐ Website
☐ Social media
☐ Traditional media, such as newspapers, television, radio
☐ Printed materials
☐ Open meetings
☐ Other:

Ensure constant, clear, and understandable communication that does not use technical language. If possible, translate the materials into all the spoken languages, and use different formats (videos, infographics, etc.) to appeal to different audiences.

Step 7: Implementing the participation process

Tip 1: Timeline

How much time do think will be needed to implement your participatory process properly?

What are the main steps, and how much time do they take?

Does the timing of the participation process align with the decision-making process?

Tip 2: Resources

How many staff (internal/external) will you need to implement the process? How many are available in your organisation?

What is your estimated budget?

Which technical resources will be needed to implement your process? Can you use existing platforms or tools?

Tip 3: Partnerships with non-governmental stakeholders

Map all potential partnerships with non-governmental stakeholders that could support the implementation of your participatory process.

Which actors could be considered allies in increasing the impact of the process?

- ☐ Civil society organisations:
- ☐ Private sector entities:
- ☐ Academia
- ☐ Media:
- ☐ Other:

Tip 4: Accessibility and inclusion

Does everyone have an equal opportunity to access and participate? Think about different personas such as parents, people with disabilities, sexual minorities, etc.

What can be done to enhance inclusivity and accessibility to the participatory process?

Tip 5: Thinking as a citizen

Review the process planned from a perspective of a participating citizen. Verify that every step is clear, inviting, inspiring confidence and trust. Some guiding questions:

- How to raise awareness about the opportunity to participate?
- How to transform awareness about the participation opportunity into interest?
- How to move from interest to actual participation and capture commitment?
- How to keep participants engaged until the end of the process?
- How to ensure they stay informed about how their input impacted public decisions?
- How to maintain their interest for future opportunities?

Step 8: Using citizen input and providing feedback

Who will respond to the participants' inputs and recommendations? What form will this take?

How will you recognise and celebrate the work of the participants?

How will you communicate the response to the recommendations? And when?

Step 9: Evaluating the participation process

How are you going to evaluate the participation process? When will the evaluation happen?

What methods will be used?

What criteria will you be using for evaluation?

Who will be responsible for the evaluation?

Step 10: Fostering a culture of participation

Think about sharing lessons learned with colleagues or an existing community of practice.

What can be done to make organising citizen participation processes easier in the future?

Can this process be institutionalised to make participation a habit?

www.ingramcontent.com/pod-product-compliance
Lightning Source LLC
LaVergne TN
LVHW061945070526
838199LV00060B/3978